Fables of Power

■ Post-Contemporary

Interventions

Series editors:

Stanley Fish and

Fredric Jameson

■Fables of Power

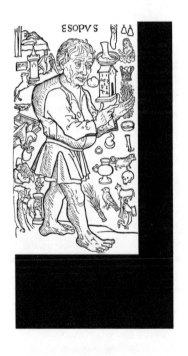

AESOPIAN

WRITING

AND

POLITICAL

HISTORY

■ Annabel Patterson

Duke University Press   Durham & London 1991

© 1991
Duke University Press
All rights reserved
Printed in the United States of America
on acid-free paper ∞
Library of Congress Cataloging-in-Publication Data
appear on the last page of this book.

▪ Contents

■ Acknowledgments

Gratitude points first to the Rockefeller Foundation, at whose Study Center in Bellagio I was a guest when this book was assembled, in idyllic circumstances. It was also facilitated by a semester's sabbatical leave from Duke University. Individuals who have contributed to it include Arthur Kinney, Gary Waller, and Gail Paster, each of whom made valuable suggestions and helped me to place my cards more squarely on the table; Dr. Josef Jařab, Barbara Herrnstein Smith, and Charles Williams, who supplied references I might not have found; Terri Clerico and Phillip Wegner, for valuable practical assistance; and Kevin Sharpe and Steven Zwicker, who not only permitted me to reprint from *The Politics of Discourse* my first essay on the politics of the fable, but provided the incentive to write it. Finally, I am grateful to my children, for being children no longer, and to my husband, Lee Patterson, whose Bellagio fellowship I was lucky to share as his spouse. Our manuscripts grew side by side on identical laptops and were finished together in congenial collaboration.

■ Introduction

It was prettily devised of Aesop;
"The fly sat upon the axle-tree
of the chariot wheel, and said,
'What a dust do I raise?' "
—Bacon: "Of Vain-Glory"

Quoting Sir Francis Bacon quoting "Aesop" quoting a fly,[1] I admit that this project, though not actually making much of little, may be thought to do so. Whenever during its development its subject has been mentioned in casual conversation, it has met with some incredulity. Everybody has been, since childhood, familiar with Aesop's fables, and almost everyone, consequently, believes them to be children's literature. As Marcel Gutwirth put it, "pedagogical practice did more than its bit in creating an indissoluble bond between our notion of childhood and our notion of fable," the latter now commonly thought of as "a place where the archaic and the puerile meet."[2] In fact, the fable's use in elementary pedagogy was only one branch of the educational practice initiated by the Renaissance humanists who recovered the great texts of classical antiquity and made them the staples of early modern philology and rhetoric. And long after the boys of the sixteenth century had been taught what they could learn from the fable as a form—grammar, the essentials of narrative fiction, the relation between moral and exemplar—they were reading and rewriting fables for their adult sagacity and cogent, real-world applicability.

This book describes the Aesopian fable as a hitherto underestimated function in Renaissance culture and subsequently. Partly thanks to their traditions of origin—how fables came to be written, by whom, and why—traditions which (whether or not

1

they believed them) were deeply interesting to sixteenth- and
seventeenth-century readers, the stories of the beasts, the birds,
the trees, and the insects quickly acquired or recovered their
function as a medium of political analysis and communication,
especially in the form of a communication from or on behalf
of the politically powerless. As Lydgate had put it for the late
middle ages:

> Of many straunge uncouthe simylitude,
>   Poetis of olde fablis have contryvid,
> Of Sheep, of Hors, of Gees, of bestis rude,
>   By which ther wittis wer secretly apprevid,
>   Undir covert [termes] tyrantis eeke reprevid
> Ther oppressiouns & malis to chastise
>   By examplis of resoun to be mevid,
> For no prerogatiff poore folk to despise.[3]

In England the tradition of political fabling was well established
by the end of the fourteenth century, when Lydgate, it is thought,
produced his own selection from Aesop and several non-Aesopian
fables. Arnold Henderson has traced an increasingly explicit tradition of social commentary in the fable from the twelfth century
through the fifteenth, culminating in those of Robert Henryson.[4]
Not coincidentally, the late fifteenth century, with its terrible history of baronial strife, also produced one of the most famous
editions of Aesop in England, William Caxton's translation of the
French version of Steinhöwel, which Caxton carefully dated as
being finished in "the fyrst yere of the regne of kyng Rychard the
thyrdde." But the period of the fable's greatest significance was
approximately the one hundred and fifty years from the last quarter of Elizabeth's reign through the first quarter of the eighteenth
century; a long historical moment whose pivot was, of course, the
English civil war, which not only provided one of the strongest
motivations for the discovery and development of new forms of
analysis, or for making old forms perform new tricks, but established for at least the next half century a structure of opposed
political values, along with a supporting symbolic vocabulary. In
the last quarter of the seventeenth century, and particularly in the
wake of the so-called Glorious Revolution of 1688, there devel-

oped what one might reasonably call a craze for political fables, whose modishness was eventually recognized by Aesop's personal transformation into a fashionable man about town.

At least for the purpose of this inquiry, it is important to distinguish the fable in the strict sense from parables, or even, more loosely, fictions. Yet the Aesopian tradition did acquire additional authority from the fact that fables, as distinct from parables, occasionally occur in scripture. Significantly, biblical (or apocryphal) fables also carry a strong political valence. In 2 Esdras 4:13–18 we are told that the angel Uriel illustrated the proper limits to human understanding by a cosmic fable:

> I came to a forest in the plain where the trees held a counsel, And said, Come, let us go fight against the sea, that it may give place to us, and that we may make us more woods. Likewise the floods of the sea took counsel and said, Come, let us go up and fight against the trees of the wood, that we may get another country for us. But the purpose of the wood was vain: for the fire came and consumed it. Likewise also the purpose of the floods of the sea; for the sand stood up and stopped them.

This early indictment of militant expansionism could clearly also be used in conservative political arguments; but a far more powerful model appeared in Judges 9:8–15, where Jotham reproached the Israelites for having made Abimelech their king. Somewhat comically, Jotham describes this event as a failed system of political nomination, whereby only the last and least qualified candidate will accept the position:

> The trees went forth on a time to anoint a king over them; and they said to the olive tree, Reign thou over us. But the olive tree said unto them, Should I leave my fatness, wherewith by me they honour God and man, and go to be promoted over the trees? And the trees said to the fig tree, Come thou, and reign over us. But the fig tree said unto them, Should I forsake my sweetness, and my good fruit, and go to be promoted over the trees? Then said the trees unto the vine, Come thou, and reign over us. And the vine said unto them, Should I leave my

wine, which cheereth God and man, and go to be promoted over the trees? Then said all the trees unto the bramble, Come thou, and reign over us. And the bramble said unto the trees, If in truth ye anoint me king over you, then come and put your trust in my shadow; and if not, let fire come out of the bramble, and devour the cedars of Lebanon.

As a threatening contrast between two types of government, and one that questioned the wisdom of the plebiscite, Jotham's clever narrative sponsored a whole series of tree fables in the seventeenth century, when the origins and sanctions of monarchy were being publicly debated, and became in its own right a commonplace of republican theory.

In certain instances, a fable could acquire a range of pertinence that gave it still greater durability. Such is the case with the famous *The Belly and the Members*, attributed to a Roman patrician of the fifth century B.C., but early assimilated into the Aesopian canon. Because it articulated in symbolic terms some of the most intransigent problems in political philosophy and practice, this fable was still going strong as a symbolic text in the mid-nineteenth century. In the seventeenth century those problems were primarily stated in terms of *natural* superiority as a basis for rule, supported by faculty psychology; the head's authority over the body, high over low, reason over the passions, was unquestionable; but whether the analogy worked in the body politic could reasonably be a matter of opinion. In the nineteenth century the analogy reappeared with a clearly capitalist and pragmatic inflection—as the need for a strong and decisive central government versus the rights of workers to participate in the system. What both formulations shared was the image of the human body and its nutritional needs as a symbol of the distribution of wealth in the body politic or socioeconomic. And what both periods shared was the recognition that the fable's meaning was not fixed but contestable, that the organicist argument had much, including custom, going for it, but that the rebellious members within the text also had a case that was constantly worth remaking.

This concept of the fable's functionality is evidently connected to my previous work on the relationship between literature and censorship in the early modern period.[5] Built into the poetics of the fable, which emerges explicitly at the end of the seventeenth century and before that, as Sir Roger L'Estrange then put it, "by Hints, and Glances," is the notion that the fable had from its origins functioned as a self-protective mode of communication, whether by a slave addressing the Master society, or by an aristocrat whose political party is currently in defeat. As L'Estrange saw it from the latter position, "Change of Times and Humours, calls for New Measures and Manners; and what cannot be done by the Dint of Authority, or Perswasion, in the Chappel, or the Closet [the authorized routes to the ears of the powerful], must be brought about by the Side-Wind of a Lecture from the Fields and the Forest."[6] When I wrote *Censorship and Interpretation*, I left the fable out of my account of functional ambiguity. I intuited that it could not be managed in a single chapter. Yet when I originally planned this present book, I made the opposite mistake. I began by thinking it would be possible to cover the fable's history, from Aesop and Phaedrus to the development of Aesopian writing in heavily censored modern cultures, and simultaneously to interrogate the most important exemplars to discover exactly how their symbolic language operated.

Obviously, this book retracts that proposition, both as overweening and perhaps not finally as useful, given the swiftness with which it would have had to move, as this much narrower study. I begin with a chapter on the legendary *Life* of Aesop, its cultural history and philosophical implications, a topic which involves such widely separated figures as La Fontaine, Hegel, and Vygotsky. But after that I confine myself and my readers to the political fable in England, and predominantly to the century and a half defined above. By so doing, it has seemed possible to write the fabulist grammar in enough detail that one can tell precisely when and how its semantic level is called into operation. In order to see, for example, what Milton was doing when he rewrote *The Belly and the Members* in his first pamphlet on church reform in the rush of intellectual excitement generated by the then brand-new Long Parliament, one needs to have a clear idea of what the "base" text of the fable was thought to be, and how it had been deployed in English culture before it occurred to Milton as a useful polemical tactic. One of those previous deployments was, of course, by Shakespeare in *Coriolanus*, itself a topic that requires extensive explication, since Shakespeare's choice of this play, and his decision to make the Belly fable its opening premise, can best be understood in the light of the major agricultural disturbances his region had just experienced, namely the Midlands Rising of 1607.[7]

I would like to think that, as well as excavating and exhibiting an important cultural artefact whose use seems largely to have been forgotten, this book could serve also as a reminder that the Aesopian tradition stands for something many people would like to forget. One of the most striking facts about the fable's history in Western culture is that Aesop and his fables appear in one of Plato's dialogues, in such a way, it might at first seem, as to grant them maximum respect. In the *Phaedo*, on the day appointed for Socrates's execution, his friends visit him in prison, and one of them asks Socrates, who had never previously composed poetry, why he had spent his time in prison producing metrical versions of Aesop's fables. Socrates replied that this peculiar behavior was a late response to the repeated injunctions he had received in dreams:

> The same dream came to me often in my past life, sometimes in one form and sometimes in another, but always saying the same thing: "Socrates," it said, "make music and work at it." And I formerly thought it was urging and encouraging me to do what I was doing already . . . because philosophy was the greatest kind of music and I was working at that. But now, after the trial and while the festival of the god delayed my execution, I thought, in case the repeated dream really meant to tell me to make this which is ordinarily called music, I ought to do so and not to disobey. . . . So . . . since I was not a maker of myths, I took the myths of Aesop, which I had at hand and knew, and turned into the verse the first I came upon.[8]

Not only does this passage provide an apparently authoritative statement that a prose version of Aesop existed at the end of the fifth century B.C.; it also places Aesop in a curiously intense and superior relation to Socrates, whose concept of wisdom he is here invoked to modify. The relation is all the more interesting in that both shared, in legend, a remarkable physical ugliness, and both were victims of an unjust execution.

That Socrates in his last days should, as a kind of spiritual insurance, have been brought to consider the Aesopian fable as what the gods had in mind—an intellectual harmony finer than that of idealist philosophy—is worth more meditation than the *Phaedo* actually gives it. It is part of the episode's silent intelligence that Socrates had himself invoked his friend's inquiry by mentioning Aesop in the context of a strong physical sensation—the removal of the fetters prior to his execution. Rubbing his leg, he proposed to his friends that pain and pleasure have themselves some mysterious physical connection:

> They will not both come to a man at the same time, and yet if he pursues the one and captures it, he is generally obliged to take the other also, as if the two were joined together in one head. And I think . . . if Aesop had thought of them, he would have made a fable telling how they were at war and god wished to reconcile them, and when he could not do that he fastened their heads together. (60:209–11)

Despite the fact that this is both a more human and a more surreal image than any included in the basic Aesopian canon, Socrates here in effect provided the first "reading" of that canon: preparing to separate his own philosophical soul from the body, and to present that separation as a manumission from a slavery *to* the body, he has nevertheless used as an instrument of that preparation the extremely corporeal and anti-idealistic fables of Aesop, the Phrygian slave.

In the long run the idealist, Platonic tradition triumphed, or, rather, chose to suppress that aspect of its own dialectic. Aesop himself was subsequently conceived not as Socrates' teacher but as Plato's antithesis, at least on the subject of education. In Richard Mulcaster's *Elementarie*, an important manifesto of Elizabethan humanism, linguistic nationalism, and pedagogic theory, Aesop became a symbolic figure of the challenge from below to the social theory of good government that the work promoted. Like so much of Tudor educational theory, Mulcaster's largest objectives were the support of public peace and the maintenance of social stratification. His third chapter, therefore, tackled the question of who in Elizabethan England deserved an education, and his answer was, not surprisingly, "chiefly . . . the principall and subaltern magistrates."[9] From the group beneath them, in order to avoid "too manie bookmen," the choice of the educable was to "respect libertie and not bondage, abilitie and not povertie, to have learning liberall, where learners be no slaves, and the execution uncorrupt, where nede is not to festur" (p. 19). By "liberall" here, which Mulcaster made cognate with his own definition of "liberty," he meant gentlemanly; by "ability" he clearly meant financial independence; and he proceeded to dispose of what might have seemed a counter-example to the Platonic barrier between education and the slave class.

In the fabulous *Life* of Aesop (described in chapter 1) the Renaissance read how intelligence could empower the disenfranchised, a lesson which Mulcaster sought severely to qualify. "And tho slaves be somtimes learned," he wrote, "yet learning is not slavish":

> neither when the parties demeanor doth procure his fredom, is learning manumised, which was never bond. Which two reasons, for libertie, and nede, the old wisdom . . . must nedes confesse, if ye look but to Aesop among slaves, & Plato among writers: whereof Aesop fought still for the fredom against servilitie, & Plato for nature against mutable fortun, measuring not even princes by their place, but by their propertie, by naturall power, and not by casuall event. (Pp. 19–21)

Thus Aesop's learning, because of its social motivation, its relation to the "casuall event," was less *valuable* than Plato's more purely speculative endeavors, which are twice identified as more "natural" than those that arise out of necessity, or the desire for personal liberty in the stronger political sense. In addition, Mulcaster wished to believe that the category of "need" could be redefined by the society. Slaves have no need for education, having "no voice nor part in the state, being held but for catle, tho reasonable withall" (p. 20). As for "abilitie," or economic power, its value as a criterion for the selection of the educated class should be "the respect of the people, which will obeie best, where theie be over topt most." And since learning has the "best voice in anie estate," it should be entrusted to only such an "utterer, as is part of the state and *capable of best state*" (p. 20; italics added). These are strong statements, probably in response to a strong and disturbing stimulus; a print culture, difficult to control; and a rapid increase in literacy and in the demand for education.

Roland Barthes's *Mythologies*, first published in 1957, a series of essays on contemporary myths and cultural icons, ends with a difficult philosophical essay, entitled "Myth Today." Discussing semiology, Barthes paused to give two examples. In the first, he imagined himself a pupil in the second form in a French *lycée*:

> I open my Latin grammar, and I read a sentence, borrowed from Aesop or Phaedrus: *quia ego nominor leo*. I stop and think. . . . I am even forced to realize that the sentence in no way *signifies* its meaning to me, that it tries very little to tell me something about the lion and what sort of name he has; . . . I conclude that I am faced with a particular, great, semiological system, since it is co-extensive with the language.

In his second example, Barthes is waiting in a barbershop, and picks up a copy of *Paris-Match*:

> On the cover, a young Negro in a French uniform is saluting, with his eyes uplifted, probably fixed on a fold of the tricolour. All this is the *meaning* of the picture. But, whether naively or not, I see very well what it signifies to me: that France is a great Empire, that all her sons, without any colour discrimination, faithfully serve under her flag, and that there is no better answer to the detractors of an alleged colonialism than the zeal shown by this Negro in serving his so-called oppressors.[10]

Subtly working these two examples together, Barthes explains how the signifier (the naming of the lion, the Negro's salute) becomes in each case a myth (for him, a negative term), by the emptying out of original meaning and replacement in another formal system:

> As a meaning, the signifier . . . has a sensory reality . . . there is a richness in it . . . it belongs to a history, that of the lion or

that of the Negro: . . . [it] could very well be self-sufficient if myth did not take hold of it and did not turn it suddenly into an empty, parasitical form. The meaning is *already* complete, it postulates a kind of knowledge, a past, a memory, a comparative order of facts, ideas, decision. . . . When it becomes form, the meaning leaves its contingency behind; it empties itself, it becomes impoverished, history evaporates, only the letter remains. (P. 117)

For Barthes, the original richness resides, in the case of *quia ego nominor leo*, in remembering the original fable from which the grammatical instance was taken: "I am an animal, a lion, I live in a certain country, I have just been hunting, they would have me share my prey with a heifer, a cow and a goat; but being the stronger, I award myself all the shares for various reasons, the last of which is quite simply that *my name is lion*" (p. 118); in other words, the Aesopian fable of *The Lion, the Cow, the Goat, and the Sheep*, which in Caxton's translation concludes with the lion's witty self-justification to his hunting companions: "My lordes . . . the fyrst part is myn be cause I am your lord / the second by cause / I am stronger than ye be / the thyrd / by cause I ranne more swyfter than ye dyd / And who so ever toucheth the fourthe parte / he shalle be myn mortal enemy." And therefore, concluded Caxton, "this fable techeth to al folk / that the poure ought not to hold felauship with the myghty."[11] For all his desire to recover the historical richness of his example, therefore, it is not clear whether Barthes remembered the social force of this fable (he slightly misremembered its participants), which would have served his argument better than he knew. At the beginning of my third chapter, I show how well it was remembered in the early seventeenth century in England, so well, in fact, that a member of the House of Commons could rewrite its text in a parliamentary debate on the royal prerogative in the full confidence that his audience would recognize the adjustments made to the original. For Barthes, the memory, slightly hazy, is preserved by a set of chances: "Time, which caused me to be born at a certain period when Latin grammar is taught; History, which sets me apart, through a whole mechanism of social segregation, from the children who do not learn Latin; pedagogic tradition, which caused this example to be chosen from Aesop or

Phaedrus; my own linguistic habits, which see the agreement of the predicate as a fact worthy of notice and illustration" (p. 119). But the most important fact has escaped him; that between Aesopian tradition, with its stress on unequal power relations, and the sign of the "Negro-giving-the-salute," which in Barthes's modern narrative are themselves merely connected by chance, lies the saving myth of Aesop the Ethiopian, black, ugly, who began as a slave but became both free and influential, a source of political wisdom. It is my hope, therefore, to make the Aesopian tradition recoverable by less chancy means than these, and to recover it definitively as an alternative to the Platonic tradition, with its strong elitist bias.

Finally, as a gesture toward the vast body of fables that were not attached to the Aesopian corpus as such, though they may have been influenced by it, I invoke the example of Leonardo da Vinci, whose library contained a copy of Aesop,[12] and whose notebooks include a small collection of extremely intelligent fables.[13] Apparently an outcome of his period of employment by the Sforzas in Milan in the late quattrocento, these fables are, as Sir Kenneth Clarke remarked, a dark reflection of Leonardo's view "of contemporary politics, and indeed of life in general, where nature only allows man to reach some pinnacle of self-esteem in order to deal him a more shattering blow."[14] Several of these are fables of personal liberty, or, more accurately, of its equivocal character; several restate the Aesopian themes of excessive ambition, or of excessive trust, in a new animal or more often vegetable key; Leonardo was particularly interested in trees. But one has a decidedly urban, contemporary edge, holding to the series the same relation as the fabulous Life of Aesop held to the Aesopian canon: that is to say, of the hermeneutical key to the code.

It is only chance, but a fine one, that as Barthes's analysis of myth began partly in a barbershop, Leonardo's fable concerns a razor:

> which, having one day come forth from the handle which served as its sheath and having placed himself in the sun, saw the sun reflected in his body, which filled him with great pride. And turning it over in his thoughts he began to say to himself: "And shall I return again to that shop from which I have just come? Certainly not; such splendid beauty shall not,

please God, be turned to such base uses. What folly would it be that could lead me to shave the lathered beards of rustic peasants and perform such menial service! Is this body destined for such work? Certainly not. I will hide myself in some retired spot and there pass my life in tranquil repose." And having thus remained hidden for some months, one day he came out into the air, and issuing from his sheath, saw himself turned into the similitude of a rusty saw while his surface no longer reflected the resplendent sun. With useless repentance, he vainly deplored the irreparable mischief, saying to himself: "Oh! how far better was it to employ at the barbers my lost edge of such exquisite keenness! Where is that lustrous surface? It has been consumed by this vexatious and unsightly rust."[15]

Leonardo partly provided his own moral: "The same thing happens," he wrote, "to those minds which instead of exercise give themselves up to sloth. They are like the razor here spoken of, and lose the keenness of their edge, while the rust of ignorance spoils their form." But he left unspoken the more trenchant application of this fable to those like himself. His razor articulates the dilemma of the intellectual whose mind has been honed to the point of aesthetic pleasure in itself, and is reluctant to waste its sharpness on what the world calls useful. It was a brilliant touch, also, to render this conceptual narcissism by making the blade its own mirror, which for lack of exercise becomes incapable of reflection ("la superfitie non vi spechiare piu lo splendiente sole"); but even more telling is the fable's candor about class, the "barbe de' rustici villani" and the "mecaniche operationi" that seem to the razor (fatally) beneath him. A good fable, too, should not corrode, but should keep itself sharp by constant application. And if Leonardo were capable of such self-consciousness in quattrocento Milan, where artists were still struggling to establish their dignity and to differentiate their products from mere artisanal work, his fable (which equally applies to those whose profession is reflection) is certainly no less pertinent today.

1 ■ Aesop's Life: Fathering the Fable

It happed that the wulf dranke above & the lambe dranke bynethe. And as the wulf sawe and perceyved the lambe he sayd with a hyghe voys Ha knave why hast thou troubled and fowled my water Which I shold now drynke. Allas my Lord sauf your grace [said the lamb] For the water cometh fro yow toward me. Thenne sayd the wulf to the lambe Hast thow no shame ne drede to curse me. And the lambe sayd My lord with your leve. And the Wulf sayd ageyne Hit is not syxe monethes passyd that thy fader dyd to me as moche. And the lambe ansuerd Yet was not I at that tyme born. And the wulf said ageyne to hym Thou hast ete my fader. And the lambe ansuerd I have no teeth. Thenne said the wulf thou art wel lyke thy fader and for his synne & mysdede thow shalt deye. The wulf thenne toke the lambe and ete hym. This fable sheweth that the evylle man retcheth not by what maner he may robbe & destroye the good & innocent man.
—William Caxton: Fables of Esope

Discussing the impact of Mikhail Bakhtin on contemporary theories of fiction, Paul de Man cited Hegel's dictum on the ancient fable: "Im Sklaven fangt die Prosa an";[1] roughly translated, "Prose originates in a slave culture." Hegel hereby granted at least the status of an aphorism to the ancient life of Aesop, father of the fable, and traditionally a hunchbacked slave of the sixth century B.C. De Man's citation, however, is not without historical irony; for Hegel's remark on the causal connection between riddling form and slavery as an institution, which De Man found valuable to connect to the ventriloquist strategies for evading censorship employed in our own century by Bakhtin, was originally, in the *Aesthetics*, merely contemptuous; and the maxim that prose began with slavery, far from anticipating the birth of the novel (as De Man implied) actually served an equation between the prosaic and the artistically primitive.

What Hegel argued was the remoteness of a fabulist mode of representation—an arbitrary and explicit comparison between an intended signified and some natural phenomenon—from the unconscious, unpremeditated union between symbol and transcendental signified he required for true art. For Hegel, the fabulist deals in mere wit, rather than depth of insight, and he restricts himself to observing such trivialities as animal habits, "because he dare not speak his teaching openly, and can only make it intelligible in a kind of riddle which is at the same time always being solved." And even Aesop's legendary place of residence, Phrygia, Hegel defined as "the very land . . . which marks the passage from the immediately symbolic and existence in bondage to Nature, to a land in which man begins to take hold of the spiritual and of [the spirit] in himself."

I begin with this misalliance between Hegel and De Man to initiate a theoretical reconsideration of the Aesopian tradition and its place in contemporary culture. If, as seems evident, the cultural value of the fable as a genre at any historical moment depends on the reigning aesthetic, and how hospitable it may be to the sociopolitical dimensions of literature, the end of the twentieth century is surely a time in which we could benefit from fabulist thinking, past and present. De Man's genial perspective, colored by the then new enthusiasm for Bakhtin, was only at the beginning of a cultural shift that has rendered again respectable "political" conceptions of literature; while the ironic relations between Soviet *glasnost* and Muslim censorship are but the most striking signs of a new international concern with the power of the literary, never more evident than when it is most threatened.

To this truth the fable bears an unusual, if not a unique relationship, thematized in several fables, but most transparently in *The Wolf and the Lamb*, which stands, in Caxton's English prose translation from the late fifteenth century, as this chapter's epigraph.[2] As England's first printer and a highly influential translator, Caxton's selection of texts for transmission in the vernacular was undoubtedly governed by the needs and special circumstances of his largely aristocratic audience. In this instance his translation carries a strong flavor of genealogical determination, ("thou art wel lyke thy fader and for his synne & mysdede thow shalt deye") that was surely appropriate for a culture struggling to understand the family feuds of the Wars of the Roses. But what that fable also tells us, perhaps more clearly today than it did for Caxton's readers, is that the declared "Moral" of unequal power relations is felt with especial poignance when language itself is seen to be helpless against that inequality, when right wins the argument but might wins the day.

Although this tragic message can obviously be countered by others from the fabulist tradition, for instance, when Chaunte-cleer, Chaucer's heroic cock in the *Nun's Priest's Tale*, literally talks himself out of the fox's mouth, the darker message of the Aesopian canon is also thematized in the figure of the Father. I refer to the tradition of the fable's origin in a slave culture, that is to say, the legendary *Life* of Aesop that typically preceded collections of fables in the late middle ages and the Renaissance. By Hegel's time that legend had already been rendered apocryphal, known to have derived from an Egyptian text of the first century A.D., to have passed through an eleventh-century Byzantine version, and to have been disseminated in two textual traditions, the first represented by the Greek *Life* attributed to Maximus Planudes, the second by the Latin translation of Rinuccio da Castiglione. Modern textual scholarship regards both strains of this tradition as having accreted the defects and lies of later periods.[3] Yet it was convenient to Hegel (and De Man) to assume that the myth still stood; and I recuperate it now as one of those rare myths of origin whose own structure implies a coherent philosophy of literature larger than itself. For the *Life* of Aesop offers us, if we read its narrative episodes thoughtfully, a set of propositions that explain what the Aesopian fable can do best, though it does not control these functions exclusively:

1. literature, in its most basic form, has always spoken to unequal power relations;
2. those without power in those relations, if they wish to comment upon them, must encode their commentary;
3. writing is authorized by authorship, texts needing a name to cling to if they are to acquire cultural resonance;
4. wit (literary ingenuity) can emancipate;
5. basic issues require basic metaphors; when, as in the fable, the role of metaphor is to mediate between human consciousness

and human survival, the mind recognizes rock bottom, the irreducibly material, by rejoining the animals, one of whom is the human body.

The ancient *Life* of Aesop was itself a complex fable whose "moral" subsumes all of these insights about itself and the genre to which it traditionally served as introduction. At first sight it might easily appear to be just a collection of old jokes, many of them scatological, strung together in a rudimentary narrative which gradually acquires an unexpected seriousness and ends badly. It has three disproportioned stages. In the first, born not only physically deformed but with a speech impediment, Aesop is miraculously given the gift of articulate wisdom in return for an act of hospitality; in the longest second phase, he is sold as a slave to a renowned philosopher, Xanthus of Samos, whom he entertains with his witty tricks, solutions to problems, and general one-upmanship. Toward the end of this phase, Aesop wearies of his role as servile prankster and begins to lobby for his freedom, which he achieves by maneuvering Xanthus into an awkward position concerning their respective abilities to interpret portents. In the third phase, having accomplished his manumission, Aesop quickly acquires an international reputation as a counselor to kings and city states, which eventually becomes his undoing; for the people of Delphi, anxious to secure their own reputation as the keepers of the oracle and correctly fearing competition from this new political soothsayer, conspire against him, have him framed for sacrilegious theft, and throw him over the cliff at Delphi into the ocean.

Judged by the standards of probability, let alone historical verifiability, this story fails. One can understand, without approving, the rationalist exasperation of Sir Roger L'Estrange, Licenser of the Press and royalist polemicist, preparing his own collection of fables at the end of the seventeenth century. L'Estrange's scholarship informed him that "it would be labour lost to Multiply Unprofitable Conjectures upon a Tradition of so Great Uncertainty. . . . For the Story is come down to us so Dark and Doubtful." And after listing a series of chronological contradictions and impossibilities from the *Life*, he concluded:

This is enough in All Conscience, to Excuse any Man from laying overmuch Stress upon the Historical Credit of a Relation, that comes so Blindly, and so Variously transmitted to us . . . it is not one jot to our Bus'ness . . . whether the Man was Streight, or Crooked; and his Name Aesop, or (as some will have it) Lochman: In All which Cases, the Reader is left at Liberty to believe his Pleasure.[4]

And there is also good sense and explanatory force in the demythologizing conclusions of Joseph Jacobs, the nineteenth-century editor of Caxton's *Aesop*, and one of the greatest deconstructors of "Aesopus auctor." Jacobs asked himself why, despite the characteristic anonymity of folktales everywhere, the Greek beast fable was connected from a very early stage with a specific personality and name, and answered his own question as follows:

> [Aesop's] was the epoch of the Tyrants, and I would conjecture that his connection with the Beast-Fable originally consisted in its application to political controversy under despotic government, and that his fate [as recorded by Herodotus] was due to the influence of one of the Tyrants with the Delphic authorities. . . . The Fable is most effective as a literary or oratorical weapon under despotic governments allowing no free speech. A tyrant cannot take notice of a Fable without putting on the cap that fits.

"Much of our ancient evidence," Jacobs continued, "points this way," and he cited Jotham's fable against Abimelech, "the Israelite *tyrannos*," and comparable fables by Theognis and Solon. And since Aesop could not have introduced the beast-fable into Greece, as it preexisted him, the only way "we can explain the later identification of his name with it is to suppose some special and striking use of the *fabellae aniles* familiar to all Greek children. Considering the age he lived in and the death he died . . . Aesop's name was associated with the Fable, because he made use of it as a political weapon."

And so, Jacobs concluded, in language that itself invokes the power of the idea it denies, "Aesop was not the Father of the Fable, but only the inventor (or most conspicuous applier) of a new use for it." That new use, he imagined (another version of Hegel's dictum on slave culture) vanished with the development of "outspoken democracies," but Aesop himself survived as "a convenient and conventional figurehead round which to gather a specialised form of the Greek jest."[5]

But such rationality has its limitations. What L'Estrange dismissed as "not one Jot to our Bus'ness" and Jacobs saw as a more or less accidental convention—the use of Aesop's name as a magnet to which all subsequent fables would be drawn—has a more than antiquarian interest. Even in Jacobs's terms, the thought that a Greek slave could be given the right, fictionally, posthumously, to a body of writing comparable in scale to other classical authors, is extraordinary. That corpus in whole or in part was edited by Aldus Manutius,[6] commented upon, among others, by Valla, Politian, and Erasmus, translated into French by Marie de France, into German by Heinrich Steinhöwel, and into English by Caxton. Steinhöwel produced the largest and most lavish edition, based on the Romulus collection supplemented by both Avianus and Rinuccio, and offered a bilingual text supported by highly influential woodcuts. First published in Ulm in 1476–77, and immediately thereafter in Augsburg, it was quickly translated into French, and it was this version, published in Lyons in 1480, that Caxton used as the base of his own translation, along with freehand copies of the illustrations, which thus became part of Aesopian tradition in England.[7]

By the end of the seventeenth century "Aesop" as the Father of the fable had become an institution. In France the appearance in 1668 of La Fontaine's Fables with his own version of the Life evidently gave the legend a new cultural significance. This resituating of Aesop at court (for La Fontaine dedicated his Fables to the six-year-old son of Louis XIV) led to the creation of an Aesopian labyrinth in the gardens at Versailles,[8] with a statue of Aesop (paired with Apollo) at the entrance (figure 1), a cogent example of reification, or the literal creation of a cultural icon.

In Restoration England there were rival illustrated editions, with the Life translated into the major European languages; and in 1687 Francis Barlow, the distinguished animal painter, collaborated with Aphra Behn in an extraordinarily lavish polyglot edition, prefaced with a new series of engravings illustrating the Life,

Figure 1. Nicolaus Visscher, The Labyrinth of Versailles (Amsterdam, 1682). Second engraving. By permission of The Folger Shakespeare Library.

and drawing "morals" from each episode, which thus became formally equivalent to the illustrated fables that follow.[9] Barlow's thirty-one designs for the *Life* were, moreover, faithfully copied by Augustin Legrand for a late eighteenth-century edition of La Fontaine's *Recueil des fables d'Esop et autres mythologistes* (Paris, 1799).[10] My point, then, is that the imaginative power of the fictional *Life* of Aesop long survived its loss of credibility as legitimate history or biography; and if it went out of circulation during the last two centuries, that fact alone might encourage us to take another look, knowing as we now do how often nineteenth-century and early twentieth-century aesthetics concealed a social agenda.

Indeed, even in antiquity it appears that there were rival interpretations of Aesop's social character and function. In Plutarch's *Symposium of the Seven Sages* (12), Aesop is one of the guests; and apart from the fact that Plutarch describes him as adviser to Croesus, king of Lydia, who did not rule until after Aesop was supposed to have died, in 564 B.C.—an anachronism that contributed to later skepticism—his character as there represented conflicts so markedly with the other ancient references that one might well suspect some revisionary intention. In contrast to the sage implied by the *Phaedo*, whose truths Socrates, himself a prisoner, might legitimately metaphrase for his own spiritual improvement, the Aesop of Plutarch is a grumpy elitist, isolated from the group by his ill will, whereas political wisdom and egalitarianism are the attributes instead of Solon. In one incident, for example, Aesop complains that their conversation ought to be more private, "lest we be accounted antimonarchical." And Solon replies reproachfully, "Do you not perceive the aim of our friends is to persuade the king to moderation, and to become an agreeable tyrant, or not to reign rather than to reign ill?"[11] Whereas this Aesop is a cynic, Solon is also the idealist in the soul-body dialectic, which, like Socrates in the *Phaedo*, he defines in terms of the Master-Slave economy: "As slaves who have gained their freedom but seldom do the drudgeries for themselves they were heretofore forced to do for their master's advantage, so the mind of man, which at present is enslaved by the body, when it once becomes free, will take care of itself, and spend its time in contemplating truth undisturbed by physical wants" (p. 249). Yet the entire discussion, and especially this Platonic commonplace, is ironized by its context—a scene of heavy eating and drinking. Suspect, therefore, on more than one account, it was Plutarch's dialogue as much as Herodotus' history that influenced the supposedly more authentic biographers of the late seventeenth and eighteenth centuries in their attempt to replace the Planudes Life, and hence to neutralize its powerful social valence.

In fact, the ancient Life of Aesop is brilliantly designed, and extraordinarily susceptible to contemporary strategies of reading. I shall cite it from Barlow's 1687 edition, as some kind of culminating statement, which in its expansions on the ancient and medieval versions of the story not only sounds distinctive, the strong voice of an early modern sensibility, but also incorporates hundreds of years of absorption of, and meditation on, the meaning of Aesop as a cultural signifier. The first issue there foregrounded (and it was one that would later be the subject of intense scholarly dispute) was that of Aesop's ugliness—a mixture of actual deformity and racial stereotypification. For "as to the Features and Dimensions of his Face and Body," we are told:

> they were so shuffel'd and hudled up, that Nature in his Production, did seem to insinuate that she oftentimes does set the most refulgent Gems in the most uneven and ragged Collets: for he was of a sharp Head, flat Nos'd, his Back roll'd up in a Bunch or Excrescence, his Lips tumerous and pendant, his Complexion black—from which dark Tincture he contracted his Name (Aesopus being the same with Aethiops) Large Belly, Crooked Bow-Legs. . . . But above all his Misfortunes, this was the most Eminent, That his Speech was slow, inarticulate and very obscure.[12]

This representation of the Other expands on the Latin text of Planudes ("Aesopus igitur, qui vitam suam, Idaeam Reipublicae Philosophicae, constituerat, & qui rebus, magis quam verbis, Philosophum egit"), but only by collating hints in the Life elsewhere; and what at first sight appears to be merely the racial prejudice of early colonialist England will shortly emerge as a crucial element in the hermeneutics of the fable. In fact the legend of Aesop's ugliness was more or less continuous, from the woodcuts in Steinhöwel's edition (figure 2) to Barlow's own engravings (figure 3); and when it was questioned (on the grounds that the classical sources do not mention it) the challenge came in a form that confirmed the social valence of the gross Aesopian body.[13]

Given these apparent disabilities, Aesop seemed inevitably born for servitude; but one day, when working in the fields, he assisted two priests of Diana and offered them food and drink. Falling asleep shortly after, he dreamed that Fortuna stood by him, "gratifying him with Volubility of Language, and the Elegancy of wrapping up his Notions under the contexture of Apologues." Leaping to his feet, he cried aloud:

> O wonderful . . . in what a charming Trance have I been engag'd! For behold I speak fluently, and by the favour of the Gods I can register each Creature by its name; this propitious Successe is the reward of my benigne Complyance with Strangers." (P. 3)

But this Adamic moment of linguistic superiority is quickly replaced by the reminder that Aesop inhabits a fallen world. Beaten by the overseer Xenas for talking back, he is then reported to his master, who perceives immediately the disruption that Aesop has brought to the local conceptual categories. "This will be ruinous to thee," he tells Xenas, "in whose Estimate he was reputed a Monster." Aesop is therefore accused by Xenas of cursing the master, and sold to a slave merchant, who sailed to Samos and there put him up for sale in the market with two fellow slaves.

This is the first opportunity for Aesop to demonstrate not just the quick wit of the trickster, but that he has a philosophical intelligence. For the slaves are looked over by Xanthus the philosopher, and when each is asked in turn what he has to say for himself, the other two make vast claims for their skills, whereas Aesop declares (with a Socratean irony) that he does not know how to do anything. Still more profound in its absolute reductiveness is Aesop's response to the question of identity:

> "Of what place are you a Native?" said the Philosopher. "I am a Negro," said Aesop. "I do not ask you this," urg'd he, "but where were you born?" Aesop answered, "Of my Mothers belly." (P. 7)

Figure 2. Heinrich Steinhöwel, trans., Esopus (Augsburg, 1477–78).
From the facsimile edited by Ernst Voullième (Potsdam, 1922).
By permission of Dartmouth College Library.

AESOP'S LIFE ■ 23

Figure 3. Francis Barlow, Aesop's Fables, With His Life (London, 1687). Facing p. 1. By permission of the British Library.

This exchange, which wins Aesop the role of the philosopher's personal servant, does much to explain the extreme corporality—others might call it grossness—that marks the early episodes of the *Life*. For Aesop works a world marked by acts of excretion, and in which body parts, especially those which Bakhtin called "the lower bodily stratum," are symbolic of human relations.[14] The *Life* anticipated Bakhtin (whose own conceptions were shaped by a repressive culture) in seeing "the material bodily principle" as a populist form; the "grotesque realism" that makes the body and its functions unforgettable is also a political statement. But the *Life* is less sentimental. Whereas Bakhtin equated scatology with a generative impulse, "the fruitful earth and the womb," the Aesopian *Life* eschews any trace of sexuality, and concentrates rather on waste; and where Bakhtin saw thematized the "collective ancestral body of all the people," the *Life* makes, paradoxically, a more cerebral statement.

Even before he was sold to Xanthus, Aesop survived a false accusation of having stolen some figs by requesting his master to try an emetic on him and his fellow slaves. Not surprisingly, it is they, not Aesop, who vomit up the contested fruit, a visible confession of their guilt. In Samos, the first sign of his new status as the philosopher's servant occurs as he and his master walk home from the market. Without pausing by the wayside, Xanthus urinates, causing Aesop to comment wittily on his master's determination not to waste time on the inessential. If one pauses oneself, even for a moment, to consider the point of this seemingly gratuitous episode, it puts in question the very category of the essential. Later, the two philosophers, master and slave, confront this question directly:

> Not long after Xanthus disburdening Nature by Seige, demanded of Aesop, why when men had evacuated their Excrements, they look'd back upon their Ordure? Aesop answered, In times foregoing a man of great effeminacy did so long engage himself in the House of Easement, that his Heart and Ordure were vented together. (P. 19)

So, he argued, all men subsequently have looked back nervously to check that the same has not befallen them. "But Sir," added Aesop, "you need not dread that this Misfortune should accrue to you, since you have no Heart at all." These three episodes, vomit, urination, and defecation, were all graphically emphasized in the woodcuts of Steinhöwel's edition; and at first sight one might be forgiven for dismissing them as the scatalogical humor associated with primitive folklore. What distinguishes Aesopian fundamentalism, however, is its source. Whereas the German folk hero Till Eulenspiegel, for example, was notorious for defecation in public places, none of the Life's excretion is performed by Aesop himself, who remains (apart from the moment of his birth) at ironic distance from it. A sign of the body's intransigence, but also its interpreter, neither its celebrant nor its despiser, Aesop exists in some indefinable category between the realist and idealist traditions.

If there were any remaining doubt that the Life encourages a philosophical reconsideration of the mind/body liaison, it should be dispelled by the episode in which Aesop, one of whose main roles is that of cook and provisioner, brings to consciousness what it means when a philosopher eats. Having been commanded to produce the best meats for a feast, he serves only tongue for every course; and when challenged to explain himself, asks rhetorically, "What does out-paralel the Tongue? This is the great Chanel by which the most refined Learning, and polish'd Philosophy is conducted down to us." And when Xanthus, seeking to protect his guests on the following day against yet more tongue, commands Aesop to produce the worst meats, not surprisingly, tongue reappears on the menu. "What," declaimed Aesop, "was worse than the Tongue? Does not the Ruine of Empires and Cities, and the Destruction of private Interests entitle itself often to its Miscarriages? Is it not the Forge of Calumnies and Perjuries? In brief, is not the whole contexture of Life disorder'd frequently by its exorbitancies?" (pp. 16–17). This literalization of a metaphor (food for thought, language as an edible organ) represents the tongue as one of the vexed points of connection between concrete and abstract; and the faint sense of culinary disgust that the tale emits only increases the vexation.

It is also a disturbing feature of the Life that one of its subthemes is a strong and grotesque misogyny. When Aesop first entered the philosopher's household, the first response of Xanthus' wife was extreme revulsion at the new slave's appearance. Even when this was overcome, there remained between them a distinct antipathy. Its climax is a famous episode in the history of embarrassment; for when the wife warns Aesop that she will always know what is happening in the household because she has eyes in her buttocks, he waits till she falls asleep, and then draws up her skirts to reveal her nakedness in front of her husband and his guests. Needless to say, Aesop's justification for this impertinence was concern that her vaunted rearguard vision should not be impeded. This episode, too, was featured in the fifteenth-century woodcut tradition, and, more surprisingly, in Barlow's Restoration engravings (figure 4) where it required from Aphra Behn an oddly apologetic feminist commentary.[15]

But, as I have said, this phase of philosophical one-upmanship, though substantially the longest section of the *Life*, gives way to another, in which Aesop rises not only above the body but also above his seemingly inevitable station. Once again, the change is initiated by providential intervention, in an episode of clearly symbolic import: "On a Day, which the Citizens of Samos had devoted to Festivity, and other Improvements of a general Mirth, an Eagle in his Flight snatch'd up the Publique Ring, and dropp'd it into the Lap of a Slave" (p. 25). The Samians consult Xanthus, as the resident *savant*, for the meaning of the portent, but he admits himself stymied. Aesop offers to interpret the sign, in return for his own manumission; but although Xanthus agrees, the Samians are initially contemptuous of his appearance. At which Aesop delivers the hermeneutic key to the *Life*, as well as to the fables it serves to introduce:

> You Citizens of Samos, you should not only view the Frontispiece of the House, but the Tenant likewise that is lodged within; for frequently, an even and compos'd Soul dwels in an uneven and disorder'd Body; for you know Men set not their value upon the exteriour Figure of the Cask, but upon the Wine concealed within.

The message anticipates that of the fable of *The Cock and the Gem*, which was frequently placed first in the collection. The analogy is between the Samians' imperception and the cock who, searching for corn in a dunghill, finds a pearl but is unable to recognize

Oft for a jest we expose our modesty,
And to assume a vertue, tell a ly,
But here deceiveing fair thou'dst small pretence,
Thy Taile wants all but the kind feeling sense.

Tho: Dudley fecit

Figure 4. Francis Barlow, Aesop's Fables With His Life (London, 1687).
Plate 17. By permission of the British Library.

its value. Implicitly a statement of the interpretive method to be used when reading fables, it also resonates with the Plutarchian account of Aesop, who was there accused by one of his fellow banqueters of having forgotten his own "fable of the Fox, who contending with the Leopard requested the umpire not to judge by outside appearances, for that he had more cunning tricks in his head than the other had spots on his skin." [16] The very attempt to represent Aesop as only concerned with externals (by calling one of his fables to witness against him) confirms the importance in Aesopian tradition more generally of an inside-outside dialectic, and hence the heuristic function of Aesop's uncouth body.

The Samians were hereby persuaded to listen to this unpersonable oracle, who informed them that, since the eagle represented monarchy, the portent seemed "to insinuate that some of the adjacent Kings will attempt to supplant your established Laws, and entombe your Liberty in Slavery" (p. 26). In return, the city praetor forces Xanthus to keep his bargain, and grant Aesop his own freedom. [17]

Here, then, is the first appearance of Aesop the fabulist, whose understanding of how birds and beasts signify was structurally connected to his other perception, that human relations are a series of negotiations between the poles of liberty and slavery. Shortly afterward his inference was proven correct. An embassy arrived from Croesus of Lydia demanding from the Samians an annual tribute unless they wished to be promptly invaded. Aesop advised against paying the tribute, on the grounds that it would only postpone and indeed initiate their capitulation:

> One Fortune (said he) hath represented to us a double expedient; one of Liberty, which in the beginning is rough and difficult, but in the Issue smooth and easie; another of Thraldome, whose beginning is easie, but the conclusion fatal and ruinous. (P. 27)

The Samians dismissed the Lydian ambassadors, who returned to Croesus with the advice that he would never subdue the Samians so long as Aesop was their counselor; and Croesus therefore proposed to the Samians that they could buy themselves out by sending him Aesop in lieu of the tribute, which they naturally found an attractive alternative.

This was the actual turning point of the *Life*, introducing the first true animal fable into the emancipatory chronology. For when Aesop perceived that the Samians were willing to hand him over to Croesus, he told them a fable whose function in the narrative he clearly specified:

> You Citizens of Samos, I am ready to prostrate my self at the feet of Croesus, but first I will rehearse one Apologue to you. In elder Times when Beasts had speech, the Wolves commenc'd a war against the Sheep, but the Sheep were secur'd by the generous protection of the Dogs; on which the Wolves employ'd an Embassie to the Sheep, the purport of which was, that if they desir'd the War should be wound up with an amiable Peace, they should resigne their Dogs; the timorous and unwary Sheep assented to this Demand, and gave up their Protectors. The Wolves immediately destroyed the Dogs, and then made the Sheep a cheap and easie Sacrifice. (Pp. 27–28)

But since Aesop had already decided that the Samians were unworthy of his counsel, this initiatory fable is self-declared inefficacious. Aesop departed for Lydia, where (by means of another fable which *was* effective) he persuaded Croesus not only to spare his own life but to make peace with the Samians; and from there he began his last fantastic phase, part counselor, part magician, first with Croesus, then King Lycerus of Babylon, and then Nectanebo of Egypt.

Yet Aesop's *Life*, or rather his death, balances his greatest successes against the suspicion that the fable is weak against injustice; or, in a more complex version of the same hypothesis, that the fable's power resides precisely in the powerlessness of those who speak its language. If we read the *Life* as capable of tragic irony, we can see that his emancipation was not the benefit it seemed, that he might have read himself the first lesson he read to the Samians, the lesson of the two expedients: "one of Liberty, which in the beginning is rough and difficult, but in the Issue smooth and easie; another of Thraldome, whose beginning is easie, but the conclusion fatal and ruinous." By having his talents appropriated to the diplomatic or recreational needs of potentates, by entering the other thraldom of wealth and influence, Aesop deprived the fable, his supernatural endowment, of its power to save himself. In the last stages of his kangaroo court execution by the Delphians, Aesop frantically, and without the slightest effect, delivers a series of fables, The Frog, the Mouse, and the Eagle, The Hare, the Hornet, and the Eagle, The Husbandman and the Asses, and finally, uncharacteristically, the all-too-human tale of a man who raped his daughter. While the first two were intended to warn the Delphians of the revenge that the gods will take upon them for Aesop's assassination, and the asses in the third fable who carry themselves and their master over a cliff are half warning, half insult, the fourth makes a sudden, last-minute amendment for the earlier misogyny of the Life, identifying Aesop now as a female victim of (literally) patriarchal violence: "She cryed out, Father, I could have chose this uncouth crime had been acted by any, rather than yourself. . . . I had rather my Fate had thrown me upon Scylla or Charybdis, or the Syrtes of Africa, than to have offer'd me up to those hands that are now ready to deprive me of Life, by so extrajudicial a violence" (p. 39).

If we read it, then, by the standards of narrative rather than biography, and of philosophical or symbolical narrative rather than those of realist fiction, the fabulous Life of Aesop tells us considerably more than merely how the fable originated, and perhaps considerably more than it is comfortable to consider. As the point of convergence of gross body and ironic wit, of liberty and slavery, of legitimate ideals of emancipation and self-destructive ambition, of sexual and political violence, Aesop functions as a test of civilized thought, as well now as when Planudes, Byzantine rhetor and theologian, or Rinuccio, Italian humanist, reshaped the ancient materials for their thirteenth- and fifteenth-century audiences. Perhaps better.

One proof of the story's significance can be seen in the various attempts, over time, to clean it up or reshape it to the needs of a less confrontational aesthetic. Caxton's illustrated edition omitted the grossest (in the excremental sense) of Steinhöwel's designs; but this was presumably simple prudery. A far more complex and indeed ambiguous instance appears in the Morall Fabillis of Esope of Robert Henryson, published in Scotland in 1570 and 1571, and based on a version of the Aesopian canon attributed to "Neveletus," now usually identified as Gualterus Anglicus, who may have been tutor to Henry II of England in the last quarter of the twelfth century.[18] Henryson offers the strongest exhibit of the psychological need to endow the Aesopian corpus with an authorial origin and presence; for in the center of his collection, as a preface to his seventh fable, he introduced Aesop himself as a dream visitor come to encourage and inspire a later, Scottish, fabulist. But this Aesop is far from ugly:

> Me thocht come throw the schaw
> The fairest man that ever befoir I saw.
> (Ll. 1347–48)

Dressed in a white gown, with a scarlet hood, white haired (and assuredly white skinned), Aesop carries a roll of paper and "swannis pen" and inkhorn:

> And said, "God speid, my sone" and I wes fane
> Of that couth word, and off his cumpany.
> (Ll. 1363–64)

In every respect this father of the fable distances himself from the Aesop of Planudes, or even of Herodotus:

> "My sone," said he, "I am off gentill blude;
> My natall land is Rome, withoutin nay,
> And in that towne first to the sculis I yude,
> In civile law study it full mony ane day,
> And now my winning is in hevin for ay.
> Esope I hecht; my writing and my werk
> Is couth and kend to mony cunning clerk."
> (Ll. 1370–76)[19]

A Roman patrician,[20] formally educated, a civil lawyer, and, finally, a Christian, Henryson's Aesop is a humanist's dream, an image not of the Other but of the writerly Self in an ideally productive, famous form. It is, of course, possible that because he received the fabulist canon through Gualterus, Henryson had somehow missed making any acquaintance with the legendary *Life*; yet one may speculate whether Henryson, like his editor, had he known that story of origins, would also have regarded it as "common (and squalid)."[21]

Fox felt it necessary to connect this urbane and respectable Aesop with Henryson's purpose in this central fable, an expanded and altered version of Aesop's tale of the sleeping lion, whose magnanimity to the mice who play round his paws while he sleeps was reciprocated by the mice when he, in turn, gets caught in the hunters' net. Henryson gave this fable a strong political turn, relating it evidently (though not clearly) to contemporary Scottish history. The sleeping lion represents the king, who is neglecting his office:

> Thir lytill myis are bot the commountie,
> Wantoun, unwyse, without correctioun;
> Thair lordis and princis quhen that thay se
> Of iustice mak nane executioun,
> Thay dreid na thing to mak rebellioun.
> (Ll. 1587–92)

And as for the huntsmen, who "waittit alway amendis for to get," Henryson drew a deliberate veil of obscurity over this part of his allegory, while insisting that further interpretation by the reader was necessary:

> For huntmen wrytis in the marbill stane.
> Mair till expound, as now, I lett allane,
> Bot king and lord may weill wit quhat I mene:
> Figure heirof oftymys hes bene sene.
> (Ll. 1610–14)

For Fox, the reconception of Aesop at this midpoint in Henryson's collection was a necessary move, authorizing the central fable's goals. Henryson's Aesop, as "a representative of Roman justice and morality, is a fit *laudator temporis acti*, and can properly give the fable a wide political interpretation, in which both the indolent ruler and the insolent commons can be condemned."[22] Yet despite his preference for a comely humanist *auctor*, Henryson did not restrict his sociopolitical analysis to the equable view from above that Fox's comments suggest. For instance, he chose to translate Aesop's *The Wolf and the Lamb*, the locus classicus of unequal power relations, which had also been one of the few selected by John Lydgate in his *Isopes Fabules*; and, like Lydgate, Henryson developed the fable into a tirade against contemporary legal injustice. Where Lydgate had complained that "shepe these dayes be spoylyd to the bon; / For there be wolfes many mo then oon, / That clyp lamborn at sessions & at shyres,"[23] Henryson inveighed against the social injustice of the Scottish system of land-ownership, in which the lamb represents the "pure pepill," "As maill men [tenant farmers], merchandis, and all lauboureris," and the wolf is subdivided into three categories of oppressors—greedy lawyers, powerful men who deprive the poor of their holdings, especially by enclosure, and the less dramatic but no less effective tyranny of those who fully exact their feudal dues, so that their tenants, in effect, "swing and sweit withoutin meit or wage . . . in labour and bondage" (p. 100).

Ideologically, therefore, it seems more likely that Henryson's choice of an identity for Aesop was based on ignorance of the *Life*, rather than a decision against it. His reading of the Aesopian canon, that part at least that he knew and chose to recirculate for sixteenth-century Scottish readers,[24] was theoretically consistent with the legend of the witty Aethiopian slave. And although his modern editor believed that Henryson eschewed topicality in his fables,[25] in fact, following Lydgate's model, he anticipated the allegorical strategies that marked the dominant fabulist tradition in England and made the fable an important medium of early modern political communication. By expanding the Aesopian fable to permit its application to local historical circumstances Henryson saw how it might be perpetually renewable; and by remarking on its privilege as a mysterious form of communication ("Mair till expound . . . I lett allane") he aligned it with a larger interpretive system, the hermeneutics of censorship.

But if Henryson's avoidance of the materialist Aesop was, perhaps, a cultural accident, the same cannot be said of the alternative biographical tradition, initiated by Claude-Gaspar Bachet, sieur de Méziriac, whose *Vie d'Aesope* appeared in 1632.[26] Méziriac rejected the fabulous *Life*, and constructed his own from the hints in classical authors, especially Herodotus and Plutarch, producing a version which erased the witty trickster but not the Aesop who consorted with the rulers of the Near East. As Robert Dodsley complained in his own nineteenth-century collection of fables, Méziriac constructed an Aesop appropriate to monarchical France:

> Méziriac, in his life of Esop, seems, like a true Frenchman, to be pleased with him for . . . his complaisance [with autocratic rule]. He says, that "his residing in the court of so mighty a king as Croesus, rendered him more polite than most of the other philosophers of his time, more compliant with the humours of princes; and more reconciled to monarchical government."[27]

Dodsley read his Méziriac via a 1704 English translation prefaced to John Toland's translation of Pierre de Boissat's *Fables . . . avec des reflexions morales*,[28] which had been published in Amsterdam in 1601. He correctly interpreted the agenda of Méziriac and his translator. Méziriac was described in Toland's preface as "a Gentleman of an antient and noble Family" (A2r); and he proved, Toland continued, that Aesop was as wise as the legendary *Life* asserted, but infinitely more dignified. For though he raised himself "from an obscure Birth and servile Condition . . . to the Dignity of a Philosopher and a States-man . . . he was a very handsome and comely Man, of an admirable quick Genius, . . . and an adroit polite Courtier, having been both a Minister and a Favourite of a mightly Monarch" (A3r).

Méziriac, then, accepted Aesop's slavery as historical fact, but emphatically denied that he was either ugly or negroid. He discredited all the legends of Aesop's service to Xanthus on the grounds of their indecorousness; for, in Toland's words, Planudes "makes him do and say so many impertinent and ridiculous things, that none can receive them for true, without imagining that Aesop was rather a pleasant Buffoon, than a grave and serious Philosopher" (p. xiii). While discarding Lycerus as unknown to the ancient authors, and Nectanebo as chronologically out of the question, Méziriac put great stress on Aesop's relation to Croesus, which (though equally anachronistic) permitted the construction of a much less threatening Author. Obviously working from Plutarch, Méziriac recounted an incident in which Aesop had pleased Croesus by excessive compliment, whereas Solon, having refrained from flattery, was coldly dismissed: "Aesop being sorry that Solon had spoken to the King with so little Complaisance, said to him . . .

O Solon, either we must not speak to Kings, or we must say what pleases them: On the contrary . . . answer'd Solon, we must either not speak to Kings at all, or we must give them good and useful advice" (p. xvi).

Dodsley was therefore cannier than he knew in defining Méziriac's Aesop as "polite"; for rather than being a "rationalist" biography, Méziriac's "true" life combines a Neoclassic aesthetic (in which the philosophical must be severed from the grotesque) and an aristocratic politics (in which the polite is defined as complaisance to the demands of "Monarchical Government"). Dodsley had begun his own career as a footman, and his first publication was *Servitude: A Poem*. His opinions, however, did not prevent him from borrowing heavily from Méziriac's "Life," and assuming that its basis in Plutarch was authentic. And (to anticipate a theme of the next two chapters) he was also exercised by the famous story recorded by Phaedrus (but not by Planudes), and which Méziriac was happy to retain, of how Aesop came to deliver the fable of *The Frogs Desiring a King*.

In Méziriac's version, "it happen'd" that Aesop passed through Athens just after Pisistratus had "usurpt the Sovereign Power, and abolisht the Popular State":

> and seeing that the Athenians bore the Yoke very impatiently, longing to recover their Liberty, and to rid themselves of Pisistratus, tho' his government was very easie and moderate, and that he was himself a very Vertuous Prince; he related to them the Fable of the Frogs that demanded a King of Jupiter, exhorting them to submit themselves voluntarily to Pisistratus, and to bear the Government of so good a Prince; lest if they depos'd him, they might chance to fall under the Power of some mischievous and cruel Tyrant. (Pp. xvi–xvii)

As we shall see, the import of this story, as of the fable itself, could vary greatly depending on the emphases of the teller; and as the social meaning of Aesop *auctor* was disputed in early modern Europe, so *The Frogs Desiring a King* also became, in its own small way, an ideological cause célèbre. Here I shall only note that Dodsley, while accepting Méziriac's account, was outraged by it:

> Esop, on this occasion, instead of inventing a Fable to shew Pisistratus how glorious it would be for him to restore lib-

erty to the Athenians; composed one to persuade that people to submit quietly to the power, which he had usurped over them . . . had not Esop been so well reconciled to monarchical government, as Méziriac thinks, and Plutarch proves he was; he would naturally have taken the part of the enslaved people, rather than that of their enslaver. (P. vi)

It was part of Dodsley's point that the "polite" Aesop was attractive (or necessary) to Méziriac as "a true Frenchman." But the politeness of Aesop in the reign of Louis XIII was a less complex construct than that required for the reign of the roi du soleil, with his theory of divinely constituted monarchy, his massively expanded court, and extensive patronage of the arts. It was for this court that La Fontaine produced both his famous fables, and a version of the fabulous Life of Aesop that was neither a rejection of Planudes nor, like Méziriac's, a new construction "tirée" from supposedly more reputable classical sources. La Fontaine engaged with the Life precisely as a fiction. In the preface to his Fables he wrote:

> It only remains to speak of the Life of Aesop. Planudes has left us one, which everybody seems to regard as fabulous. The common supposition is that this author set out to invent for his hero a character and adventures in harmony with his Fables. I used to think this notion specious, but as time goes on I believe in it less and less. It is chiefly based on Aesop's dealings with Xanthus, which are thought too full of absurdities to be true. But where is the Sage to whom such things do not happen. . . . All that I could do would be to weave a web of my own conjectures and call it the Life of Aesop. However plausible I might make it, no one would be taken in, and fable for fable, the reader would always prefer Planudes' to mine.[29]

As Marie-Christine Bellosta has argued, this refusal to contest Planudes' authority was not solely caused by a reaction against the "hypercriticism" of Méziriac or the desire to recirculate an amusing tale. The Life interested La Fontaine because it preserved, for him, the essentials of the Aesopian tradition;[30] and he grasped, perhaps all the more securely because of Méziriac's imperception, that the fabulous Life of Aesop had been written so as to serve, not only as the first fable in the collection, but as the metafable which should govern the interpretation of the whole.[31]

La Fontaine, however, did not retain in his version of the *Life* those early episodes which, for me, constitute the essential Aesop —the philosopher of materialism and the body—before his emancipation. La Fontaine erased for his own polite purposes the excremental episodes,[32] the exposure of Xanthus's wife, and all the scenes in which Aesop plays with words, with the notable exception of the dinners of tongues. For La Fontaine, Aesop is not to be understood in the tradition of Diogenes or of the Socrates of Diogenes, but as the philosopher of language. According to Bellosta, this ironic concern with language mocks the rationalist tradition even as it discards the skeptical one. As the supplement attached to the sense of powerlessness that overtakes rationalism when it tries to interpret the world, the Aesopian fable, she argued, presents that world as a proliferation of meaning, of excessive or surplus signification.[33] But Bellosta's deconstructive critical vocabulary, which implies a philosophical critique of referentiality, of the capacity of literature to specify extratextual concerns, seems inconsistent with her other contention, that La Fontaine read out of the *Life*, and hence of the Aesopian fable as a whole, a political message: that the fable was a ruse employed by the underprivileged for survival in a hostile world.[34] This may well have been La Fontaine's perception in France in the 1660s. Bellosta believed that his reproduction of the *Life* was a confession of the underlying pessimism invisible through the polished surface of his fables; yet one must add that this finish, while it still permitted a political interpretation for some of his fables,[35] shifted the genre and subsequent criticism of it toward problems in aesthetics.

Theoretical discussion of the fable *as* a problem in aesthetics began with La Fontaine and passed through Lessing and other aestheticians to Russian Formalism. In essays subsequently published in *The Psychology of Art*, L. S. Vygotsky attempted to account for the effectiveness of the fable as a genre in terms of "the rules of art," by searching in each tale's interior narrative dynamics not for its grasp of fundamental power relations but instead, by what now seems an act of determined repression, for some formal principle for the distribution of energy. This approach, it scarcely needs saying, is one with which I profoundly disagree; yet the very historical irony that created Russian Formalism as a defense against state-enforced standards of realism and functionalism in literature should serve as a warning against anything so complacent as mere theoretical disagreement. Vygotsky's arguments, too, came unfortunately to the attention of the anglophone reader only in the early 1970s, when formalism was perceived as, if not discredited, temporarily exhausted, and they thus achieved instant obsolescence.

Vygotsky began his analysis from Lessing's perception that, thanks to La Fontaine, the fable, which had previously belonged to the territory of philosophy and rhetoric, had decisively entered literary history; or rather, La Fontaine's contributions to the genre seemed to Vygotsky to require a formal distinction between the short fable, usually in prose, and the more elaborate confections which clearly deserved their own poetics. But whereas Lessing had intensely disliked La Fontaine's fables for this poeticization, Vygotsky reversed that judgment. Not having within his critical repertory the concept of *aestheticization*, Vygotsky was unable to deal with the shift that had evidently taken place in the fable except by the crude and misleading contrast between prose and verse, a contrast that ignored the extraordinary history of the Aesopian canon and its constant redactions from prose to verse and back again. If nothing else, Plato's story in the *Phaedo* of how Socrates set himself the task of versifying Aesop's truth might have warned Vygotsky that, philosophically speaking, the fable's value or function was not to be defined by the presence or absence of meter; and that a single fable such as *The Wolf and the Lamb* could appear sometimes in a brief prose version, sometimes, as in Henryson, in an expansively poetic (though by no means necessarily aestheticized) form. But for Vygotsky the consequence of beginning his inquiry with La Fontaine, instead of with Phaedrus, for example, was a peculiarly narrow definition of the subject under inquiry—the internal mechanics of what he called the "lyrical" fable and I call its "polite" extension.

Vygotsky's other chosen problematic was the relation of the fable to its stated moral. He noted, as commentators have often done, that the articulate moral of a fable is not always the inevitable or the only conclusion to be drawn from the event narrated, and that, conversely, a single moral may be illustrated by more than one fabulist plot, some of which may be, mysteriously, more effective than others. Again, Vygotsky took his cue from La Fontaine, who had himself seen a theoretical problem here, and presented it as another form/content or body/soul dilemma:

> After establishing . . . the moral as the soul of the fable, La Fontaine is forced to admit that frequently he has to prefer the body to the soul. Occasionally he must even do away with the soul when it does not fit the story and disrupts the grace of the form. . . . Does this mean that the moral was confined only to the prosaic stories and had no place in the lyrical fable? As a first step, we have to establish that a lyrical story does not depend on the moral in its logical trend and structure.[36]

For his test case, then, Vygotsky turned to The Wolf and the Lamb, as Lessing had done before him, and before him, Batteux. All three in sequence complain that the articulate moral is insufficient to motivate the fable. In Batteux's words: "the moral which we gather from this fable is that the weak are frequently harassed by the powerful. How trite! How insincere! If this fable taught us nothing else, it would seem perfectly useless for the poet to have invented the 'insincere' arguments of the wolf."[37] Vygotsky also cites approvingly Napoleon's complaint, generated by La Fontaine's version of the fable, that it is actually immoral, that it "violates the principle of morality . . . it is unjust que la raison du plus fort fût toujours la meilleure" (p. 110), a remark that obscures the issue by shifting the meaning of "moral" from realist observation to idealist prescription. But Vygotsky's chief objective was to free the narrative structure from any genetic dependence on the moral— that is to say, its social meaning—in order to develop his formal premise—that the energy of the fable derives from a principle of tension, antithesis, or contradiction. "We shall always find," he wrote, "superfluous elements, such as the invented accusation of the wolf, which are completely unnecessary for the expression of a commonplace idea" (p. 107):

> Apparently, however, the whole point of the story is in those false accusations moved by the wolf against the lamb. Thus, the action in the fable moves continually on two levels. One is the "juridical oppression," and there, the odds are obvi-

ously in favor of the lamb. Every new accusation of the wolf is promptly and successfully countered. . . . But with each reply, the lamb, in justifying his position, moves closer to his doom. At the point of culmination the wolf runs out of argument, both trends join, and victory on one level results in defeat on the other. In this carefully devised system, feelings are evoked on one level which are diametrically opposed to those evoked on the other. This fable seems to tease our emotions. With each new justification of the lamb we hope that his fate will be averted, while in reality he comes ever closer to his death. (P. 121)

Despite the emphasis on a "carefully devised system" and on diametrical opposition, Vygotsky was perhaps aware that his brilliant redescription of the fable was actually empowered by a psychosocial sympathy that could not be effectively severed from its experiential connections in the world; and in the last phase of his argument, which involves an account of Russia's most famous fabulist, Ivan Krylov, Vygotsky attempted to render his account more objective by using the analogy of scientific energy: "The catastrophe (or *pointe*) of a fable is its concluding phase, in which the contrasts and contradictions are driven to the extreme, and the emotions that built up in the course of the fable are discharged. There occurs a short-circuiting of the two opposing currents. The contrast explodes, burns, and dissolves" (p. 142).

Vygotsky's determination to deprive the fable of its sociopolitical semantics was, as I have said, understandable in terms of Soviet history, and hence of Soviet literary theory. The irony of his position, however, became both more explicit and more desperate when the exhibit was not an ancient fable rewritten by La Fontaine but a modern one written for his own nation out of their recent historical experience. For one of the fables of Ivan Krylov with which Vygotsky chose to illustrate his theory was *The Wolf in the Kennel*, which had always been understood as an account of Napoleon's invasion in the war of 1812, and was said to have been claimed as such by Kutuzov, the general who had successfully trapped the invading army after the battle of Borodino by allowing the French to enter Moscow. In Krylov's fable a marauding wolf finds himself in a kennel of hounds and, like the lamb in Aesop's fable, tries, without real hope, to talk himself out of a desperate situation:

> He saw that this was different from
> The fields and woods. He saw
> The reckoning before him for all the sheep
> He'd killed, and he decided, cunningly,
> To start discussions.[38]

Without noting the significance of Krylov's reversal of the ancient symbolic system, Vygotsky determined that the power of *The Wolf in the Kennel*, too, derived from contradiction. But what it could not, in his system, draw on for its emotional force and complexity was the investment of the Russian reader in the historical event. "We will not," wrote Vygotsky, "go into the complicated problem of determining whether this speculation [as to the fable's occasion] is true:

> All we will say is that no historical motive will explain anything in the fable. A fable created for any reason or purpose follows its own rules and is governed by its own requirements; and these rules and requirements can never be explained by a mirror image of historical fact or reality. At best, history may be a starting point for our speculations . . . but it will never be anything more. (P. 133)

This book of mine, however, is based on the opposite premise; that without a lively engagement with history as an interpretive frame for the Aesopian fable in its passage through time the genre will seem as dead as Marcel Gutwirth feared.[39] Put more strongly and positively, the fable demands a more satisfying account of cultural energy than that implied by Vygotsky's electrical poles. Once reestablished in late medieval and early Renaissance Europe, and especially as glossed by the initial metafable of Planudes' *Life* of Aesop, the fable changed, dramatically and constantly, to meet the cultural needs of societies themselves in rapid and often alarming transition. From the last quarter of the fifteenth century to Krylov's fable in 1812/13, social and political analysis was frequently conducted, bizarre though that practice may now seem, in a symbolic vocabulary that could still be called Aesopian even when, as was the case for The Wolf in the Kennel, the symbolic counters had been arranged and the new plot was entirely topical. And because historical circumstances were, not always but often, the compelling motive for translation, paraphrase, commentary, or straightforward innovation, a historicized poetics of the fable has the double advantage of allowing us to read in both directions. The fable gives up its goods more generously when its details are recognized as specifying, not generalizing; and those details, in turn, constitute an unusual and untapped archive for the early history of political and social thought.

2 ■ Fables of Power: The Sixteenth Century

O wretch that thy fortunes should moralize
Esops fables, and make tales, prophesies.
Thou'art the swimming dog whom shadows cosened,
And div'st, neare drowning, for what's vanished.
—John Donne: Satire 5

The history of the fable in the sixteenth century is, from one perspective, continuous with that of the late middle ages. John Lydgate's *The Horse, the Goose, and the Sheep*, which included comments on the fable's function as a medium of communication, "under covert," of social protest by the poor and their advocates, was printed by Caxton in 1477, and by Wynkyn de Worde in 1499 and again in 1500. Lydgate's *The Churl and the Bird* was, likewise, printed by Caxton in 1478 and by De Worde in 1520. The latter poem, claiming to be a translation from a French "pamphlet" and indeed an expansion of a clerical fable by Petrus Alfonsi,[1] becomes in Lydgate's treatment an extended meditation on the fable tradition in the world of political power structures, especially in its relation to freedom of expression.

For *The Churl and the Bird*, whose center is a Chauntecleer-like tale of how a captured bird outwitted her captor, is, quite unlike the *Nun's Priest's Tale*, a moving account of the problems of poets who are forced to operate under any kind of social constraint, from clientage to more extreme forms of repression. (Lydgate himself wrote to order for Henry V, Henry VI, and Humphrey, duke of Gloucester, and *The Churl and the Bird* ends by recommending itself "unto my maister.") Having trapped the bird, the churl (peasant) "cast for to make, / Withyn his hous a praty litel cage, / And with hir song to rejoissh his corage." But here is the bird's response:

> I am now take & stond undir daungeer,
> Holde streite, & I may not flee;

Adieu my song & al my notis cleer
Now that I have lost my liberte,
Now am I thral, and sometyme I was fre,
And trust weel now I stonde in distresse,
I can-nat syng, nor make no gladnesse.

And thouh my cage forged were of gold,
And the pynaclis of beral & cristall,
I remembre a proverbe seid of old,
"Who lesith his fredam, in soth, he leseth all;
For I have lever upon a braunche small,
Meryly to syng among the woodis grene,
Than in a cage of silver briht and shene.
Song and prisoun have noon accordaunce,
Trowistow I wole syngen in prisoun?

     · · · · ·

Ryngyng of ffeteris makith no mery soun,
Or how shold he be glad or jocounde
Ageyn his wil that lith in cheynes bounde?[2]

In addition, Lydgate opened his fable with several metacritical stanzas that implicitly relate this central issue to the "liknessis & ffigures" with which, from time immemorial, fables have been constructed. Beginning with Jotham's fable, in Judges 9, of how the trees of the forest went about to choose themselves a king, Lydgate proceeded to the secular tradition in which monarchy involves consideration of parliamentary government:

And semblably poetes laureate,
Bi dirk parables ful convenyent,
Feyne that briddis & bestis of estat—
As roial eglis & leones—bi assent
Sent out writtis to hold a parlement,
And maade decrees breffly for to sey,
Some to have lordship, & som to obey.
(2:469)

These poems today exist on the fringes of "literature," as supposedly minor productions of a poet whose reputation has faded into insignificance beside Chaucer. Yet their history of publication in the fifteenth century and early sixteenth century implies that their message was noticed and valued, that it carried an application to early Tudor England. It seems inarguable to me that Lydgate established an English tradition of political fabling as a form of resistance to unjust power relations, which ran continuously alongside (or beneath) the more conventional and conservative notion that the content of fables was merely ethical, and that they could, therefore, serve as benign texts in the elementary education of children. Lydgate's reminder in *The Churl and the Bird* that "Poetes write wondirful liknessis, / And under covert kept hem silf ful cloos" (2:469), was, as we shall see, a cardinal principle of sixteenth- and seventeenth-century fabulists.

Yet the established critical position has been that the fable does not or should not do what Lydgate believed it had always done. Rather, we have been told, it should eschew topicality (or political allegory) and speak to the most general (and hence socially neutral) moral concerns. As Lessing remarked in his *Abhändlungen über die Fabel*, published in 1759, "the fable only becomes an allegory when to the invented individual case which it contains [the animal plot] a similar and real one [of human, historical circumstance] is added; and the word allegory must be regarded as not at all connected with the strict definition of the fable, which in its essence ought to convey a general moral precept." [3] This eighteenth-century opinion remains as an uninspected premise in modern criticism of the fable, reinforced by other prejudices—against allegory as a mode of figuration and against historical circumstances as a subject of representation or an object of interpretation—inherited respectively from Romanticism and New Criticism. Denton Fox's desire to ignore the evident topicality of Henryson's fables [4] is related to Derek Pearsall's critique of Lydgate's. For Pearsall, Lydgate's fables are only of interest insofar as they can be compared, unfavorably, to Henryson's, as in their common interest in *The Wolf and the Lamb*. Henryson is praised for his development of narrative as distinct from its moralization and for "realism, the sense of a significance attaching to life in its literary imitation." Lydgate's handling of the fable is described as "bookish, moralistic, typically medieval," and although the further charge of "quietism" is leveled, you would never elsewhere guess from Pearsall's description that Lydgate's fables were driven by political actuality, were everywhere concerned with what Lydgate calls "tyranny," especially in the legal system.

More telling still is the comparison, again unfavorable, with Chaucer. Chaucer is praised for "his gradual sloughing-off of the externally imposed moralisation" endemic to fable tradition:

> The Nun's Priest's Tale explodes the fable in a cascade of literary fireworks, so that the mock-serious injunction at the end, "Taketh the moralite, goode men," can evoke the bewildered response, "Which one?" The moral is mortified into absurdity and irrelevance, and our attention directed back to the body of the tale. . . . In the Manciple's Tale Chaucer provides as the moral a string of unctuous platitudes which reflect back not upon the tale but upon the narrator, and upon the whole concept of the fable as a vehicle of moral wisdom. These very platitudes, parodied by Chaucer, are presented by Lydgate with a perfectly straight face.[5]

If one starts, however, with a bias in favor of political consciousness, it greatly enhances one's capacity to recognize its presence. And in fact Chaucer's fables clearly contain their own brand of politics. The Nun's Priest's Tale of Chauntecleer's escape from the fox may avoid explicit social commentary (which in Pearsall's vocabulary is not distinguished from moral platitude), but it gratuitously expresses contempt for "Jakke Straw and his meynee" (l. 3394), Chaucer's only reference to the Peasants' Revolt of 1381. The early Parliament of Fowls completely suppresses from the idea of a "parliament" any political implications; it is merely the forum for aristocratic dynastic-marital disputes; and the Manciple's Tale anticipates Lydgate's use of the caged bird motif, in language that Lydgate evidently remembered:

> Taak any bryd, and put it in a cage,
> And do al thyn entente and thy corage
> To fostre it tendrely with mete and drynke
> Of alle deyntees that thou kanst bithynke,
> And keep it al so clenly as thou may,
> Although his cage of gold be never so gay,
> Yet hath this brid, by twenty thousand foold,

Levere in a forest, that is rude and coold,
Goon ete wormes and swich wrecchednesse.
For evere this brid wol doon his bisynesse
To escape out of his cage, yif he may.
His libertee this brid desireth ay.
(Ll. 163–74)

Yet having admitted the problem of constrained speech, Chaucer's tale decides against the bird and against freedom of expression. The manciple's fable of the crow, once white but transformed to black by Apollo for betraying the adultery of its mistress, concludes with a moral precisely the opposite of Lydgate's theory of the fable. In fifty lines Chaucer's manciple repeats over and over the injunction to silence:

My sone, be war, and be noon auctour newe
Of tidynges, wheither they been false or trewe.
Whereso thou come, amonges hye or lowe,
Kepe wel thy tonge, and thenk upon the crowe.
(Ll. 359–62)[6]

It might be possible to argue that the manciple is mocked for Polonius-like sententiousness; but there is nothing in the *Manciple's Tale* to suggest that its *message* is to be held suspect. It appears that Chaucer did what he could to neutralize the fable's potential for protest or resistance and that Lydgate did what he could to reverse the process.

Early Tudor writers had reason continually to assess these rival models. In the 1520s John Skelton developed the model of the bird in the cage with unsurpassed brilliance, but not without a certain equivocation between the extremes of outspokenness and silence. *Speke, Parott* is a tour de force of vituperation directed against Cardinal Wolsey, in which the conceit of a truly talkative bird who is nevertheless a court pet and learns by rote permitted Skelton to encode some of his most violent accusations in a seemingly random medley of foreign tongues:

For trowthe in parabyll ye wantonlye pronounce
Langagys divers; yet undyr that dothe reste
Maters more precious than the ryche jacounce.
(Ll. 363–66)[7]

Yet, as Arthur Kinney has shown, the complexity of Skelton's biblical sources renders the fabulist plot almost invisible in a far more learned project. His Parrot, in fact, "pretendith to be a bybyll clarke" (l. 119).[8]

At about the same time Wynkyn de Worde had printed, as well as Lydgate's *The Churl and the Bird*, an anonymous *Parliament of Birds*, which may also have been intended as anti-Wolsey persuasion. In sharp distinction to Chaucer's poem with a similar title, this *Parliament* makes no bones about the institution's political function:

> This is the parlyament of byrdes,
> For hye and lowe and them amyddes,
> To ordayne a meane: how it is best
> To keepe among them peace and rest,
> For muche noyse is on every side
> Agaynst the hauke so full of pride.
> Therfore they shall in bylles bryng
> Theyr complaint to the egle, theyr kyng;
> And by the kynge in parlyament
> Shall be sette in lawful judgement.[9]

In fact, the poem divides into two complaints, one against the hawk, represented as a gray-headed chief minister of the realm, and the crow, an upstart who has received, with the eagle's initial encouragement, borrowed feathers from each of the birds to permit him to come to attend the parliament in proper array. Eventually this arrangement causes more outrage than the crow's initial absence, and is consequently reversed:

> Then was plucked fro the crowe anone
> All his feders by one and by one,
> And lefte in blacke instede of reed.
> (P. 66)

It is possible that this episode refers, by way of allusion to the red of the cardinal's robe, to Wolsey's fall in 1529, which was also the year of the Reformation Parliament; but a more interesting form of political commentary is represented by the hawk, whose role in the poem is less to defend himself than the system as it stands, and especially to articulate the position of Chaucer's *Manciple's Tale*, against freedom of speech:

The hauke answered the prating pye:
"Where is many wordes the trouth goeth by;
And better it were to seace of language sone,
Than speake and repent whan thou hast done."

Than sayd the sterlynge: "Verament,
Who sayth soth shal be shent;
No man maye now speke of trouthe
But his heed be broke, and that is routhe."

The hawke swore by his heed of graye:
"All sothes be not for to saye:
It is better some be left by reason,
Than trouthe to be spoken out of season."

Than spake the popyngeiay of paradyse:
"Who saythe lytell, he is wyse,
For lytell money is sone spende,
And few wordes are sone amende."

The hawke bade: "For drede of payne
Speke not to moche of thy soverayne,
For who that wyll forge tales newe
Whan he weneth leest his tale may rewe."
(P. 60)

Echoes of this debate would be heard in the The Mirror for Magistrates in the years following Elizabeth's accession,[10] in Spenser's
Shepheardes Calender, and Sidney's Arcadia, and, from the perspective
of the hawk, in Lyly's Euphues his England. But by the end of the
century this thematic continuity would have seemed less obvious, perhaps, than a newly ratiocinative and applied approach to
the fable. John Donne took it for granted that a fabulist mode of
reference was a necessary part of the thinking man's intellectual
machinery. The fifth of his satires, quoted as this chapter's epigraph, concluded with an appeal to the typical late Elizabethan,
trapped in a world of entrepreneurial greed and humbug, and seeing himself in Aesop's Dog and the Shadow. One of the most famous
of his verse letters, The Calme, begins with a metaphor that equally
depends on familiarity with the Aesopian fable, in this instance the
famous Frogs Desiring a King. "The fable is inverted," wrote Donne of

his voyage to the Azores in 1597, "and farre more / A blocke afflicts, now, then a storke before." The first poem printed in the 1633 edition of Donne's poems was Metempsychosis, an amalgam of the ancient animal fable with its related concept of metamorphosis, the whole underwritten by Pythagorean notions of the transmigration of souls, but the purpose political satire.[11] And in one of his epigrams Donne identified himself as "Esops selfe," the man of wisdom who recommends himself for sale in the slave market by admitting he knows nothing, whereas his fellow slaves profess omnicompetence.[12] The metaphor derives from one of the earliest episodes in the Life of Aesop, and speaks to that text's continual contrast between conventional values and alien insights, wisdom from below.

I take this congeries of allusions to indicate that the second half of the sixteenth century in England was the time (and place) where the Aesopian fable entered early modern culture decisively. In Donne's practice the details of fable plots were not merely an educational residue, a reminder that boys in the grammar schools would probably read Aesop as their first classical author. In Donne's glancing allusions the fable was evidently a reflex of the political imagination; and in other hands (Sidney and Spenser) it had already become the medium in which opposing political theories were debated with considerable precision and even, perhaps, constructed. It is also evident that throughout the early modern period writers who reused the Aesopian materials frequently consulted their English predecessors, and conducted their debates with their support or against their opposition; which is not to say that the literary system operated solely by the mechanism of internal reflexes. On the contrary, it appears that the relation between old forms and their new application to events in the real world was taken so seriously that later fabulists consulted earlier ones as carefully as if they were historians or political philosophers.

In the last decades of the sixteenth century there were created in England the conditions that promote Aesopian writing in the looser modern sense; that is to say, a flexible and constantly renewable system of metaphorical substitutions for actual events, persons, or political concepts that can, but need not, be recognized as such. Among those conditions were a great increase in formal education (including, of course, access to the ancient fabulists); a large group of dissatisfied intellectuals, like Donne himself; and, perhaps most importantly, a determination by the authorities (the queen and her privy council) to exert political control over all the public media of expression at a time when the spread of print technology made such control more difficult, and therefore more obvious in its legal manifestations and public justifications.

The result was a steadily increasing tendency to recuperate not only the fable as a genre, but the genre's own political history, as implied in the *Life* of Aesop and by Phaedrus. Thus certain ancient fables, *The Dog and the Wolf*, which Phaedrus had identified as a liberty-text, or *The Frogs Desiring a King*, which Phaedrus attributed to Aesop on the occasion of a coup by Pisistratus in Athens, inevitably carried with them their original historico-political context, which allowed them to become both exemplars of how to construct a topical fable and permanent tropes in the public discourse of early modern Europe. Others, particularly those that featured the lion, quickly became metaphors for the strengths and limitations of monarchical government in emergent nation states. And still others, like the famous fable of *The Belly and the Members* attributed to Menenius Agrippa and reported both by Livy and Plutarch became, as in Shakespeare's *Coriolanus*, an extremely complex text in which even the tiniest verbal variations could become the bearers of an individual political posture.

Also, a great deal of formal innovation took place within the fable as a genre. It could be massively expanded into a longer narrative, as, for example, by Edmund Spenser in *Mother Hubberds Tale*, one of the chief models for John Dryden's *Hind and the Panther* a century later. Expansion could also be dramatic rather than narrative. In the first decade of James's reign Ben Jonson refashioned the many fables that featured a quick-thinking fox into the plot of *Volpone*, producing an astringent but morally ambiguous analysis of Jacobean legacy hunters, parasites and catamites, professional politicians, and ultimately the entire legal system.[13] No one did more, in the mid-seventeenth century, to expand the fable's possibilities as local political commentary than John Ogilby, in whose hands Aesopian originals became at once definitively lyrical (as distinct from merely being versified) and definitive markers of both civil war and Restoration thinking; yet Ogilby too looked back to Spenser for technical innovation, while enlisting the fable as far as was possible to the support, rather than the critique, of the monarchy then in defeat or exile.

It is one of the fable's habits (and this book's objectives) to oscillate between "literary" exempla and others not normally thought of as literature. If a by-product of this chapter is a clearer sense of what that distinction means and whether it can be maintained, so much the better; but the chief objective is to show the habit itself, the deep penetration of the fable into the culture. I begin with a striking example that itself straddles the divide. In July 1586 there was discovered a Roman Catholic plot against Elizabeth by young aristocrats led by Anthony Babington; the leaders were all executed in September in a public spectacle, complete with the full horrors of disembowelment; and early in 1587 there was rushed into print a new edition of "Holinshed's" Chronicles. Though Raphael Holinshed himself was dead, a committee of antiquaries including John Stow continued the history of England through Elizabeth's reign and literally up to the moment. Its conclusion was devoted to an account of the Babington plotters, their discovery and trial, and the public satisfaction at the rigors of the punishment. The chronicle described how, in the Tower, the conspirators "occupied their wits in dolorous devises . . . savouring more of prophane poetrie than christianitie, of fansie than religion"; and Babington, in an appeal for clemency on the basis of his rank, managed to distribute certain poems, which were promptly illegally printed: "the copies are common (yet never authorised for the print)."

The chronicler continued:

> Furthermore, . . . to procure the speedier commiseration (in his fansie) he falleth into a familiar tale of a certaine man, that having a great flocke of sheepe, mooved either with a sheepish unruliness, or for his better commoditie, threatened everie daie by one and one to dispatch them all: which he dailie performed according to his promise, untill such time as the terror of his accustomed butcherie strake the whole flocke into such a fear, as whensoever he came and held up his knife, advising at that instant but the slaughter of one, the

whole number of them would quake, fearing each one his particular chance. Which tale he applieth to himself, being one of the brutish herde (as he confesseth) that for their dis- ordinat behaviour the law justlie condemneth, and threatneth to dispatch one after another.[14]

This extraordinary insert, marked out for readerly interest, in- deed, *literary* attention, by the marginal gloss "A fable or tale which Babington applieth to his present case of wretchednesse," demon- strates with a fearful economy all but one of my opening postulates about how the fable functions in the world. Clearly, it speaks to unequal power relations, and to the need for those without power in those relations to encode their commentary upon them, not to preclude understanding, but in order to claim for their protest the sanction of an ancient form; and equally clearly, Babington hoped that wit or literary ingenuity (which the chronicler degraded as "fansie") would emancipate him, save him from the Tower and the scaffold.

The chronicler assumed this to be "a familiar tale." In fact, it was a remarkable adaptation of the Aesopian fable of *The Sheep and the Butcher* which appeared in Steinhöwel's edition (and hence also in Caxton's) with a woodcut showing the butcher cutting the throat of one sheep while the rest of the flock look on (figure 5). The moral of the original fable was that personal safety depends on group solidarity. In Caxton's translation the fable reads as follows:

> Whenne a lygnage or kyndred is indyfferent or in dyvysyon not lyghtly they shalle doo ony thynge to theyr salute as re- herceth to us this fable Of a bocher whiche entryd within a stable full of whethers. And after as the whethers sawe hym none of them sayd one word. And the bocher toke the fyrst that he fonde. Thenne the whethers spake al to gyder and sayd lete hym doo what he wylle. And thus the bocher tooke hem all one after another sauf one onely. And as he wold have taken the last the poure whether sayd to hym Justly I am worthy to be take by cause I have not holpen my felawes. For he that wylle not helpe ne comforte other ought not to demaunde or aske helpe ne comforte. For vertue which is uny[t]ed is better than vertue separate.[15]

Figure 5. Heinrich Steinhöwel, ed., Esopus (Augsburg, 1477). From the facsimile by Ernst Voullième (Potsdam, 1921). By permission of Dartmouth College Library.

Caxton's translation had been telling in its own time, in its substitution of "lygnage or kyndred" for the Latin "Parentes vel amici," thus appealing to precisely that standard of loyalty based on lineage in an honor culture that was already being eroded, as much by the internecine Wars of the Roses as by the long international development of centralized monarchies.[16] And in 1484 this fable would have had a specific, horrific charge, published as it was the year after Richard III took over the throne, an event accomplished by the summary executions of Earl Rivers and Lord Hastings, not to mention the probable murder of the young king Edward V and his brother.

But whereas Caxton was content to let the fable do its work in 1484 with only minimal adjustment to the circumstances, Babington, through the voice of the chronicler, had apparently rewritten the fable so as to add to its "familiar" message an unmistakable indictment of the psychology of repression. Caxton's sympathy for the "poure whether" and the brutal implications of "bocher" are retained, which already ran counter to the sheep's confession that he suffered justly for his earlier passivity, for nonintervention in the deaths of his colleagues; but he nowhere anticipated the brilliance of Babington's conception whereby the shepherd terrifies his flock into submission by a daily, ritual execution of one of their number. This was a genuine insight into the Elizabethan theory of public executions as, literally, exemplary ritual; a theory to which, of course, the 1587 *Chronicles* subscribed or claimed to subscribe.[17]

Yet however much the law-and-order mentality of the narrator attempts to control the fable's power by editorial comment, the story transmits its own message. A "sheepish unrulinesse" (which is only hypothetical, and may actually be an excuse for the shepherd's "better commoditie") scarcely justifies such "accustomed butcherie" as indeed, common sense asserts, must surely work *against* the economy of sheep farming; while the metaphor itself has disturbing implications for the idyllic versions of pastoral, with the queen as shepherdess, which were already fashionable in Elizabethan courtly poetry and drama.

Today's reader can therefore speculate on the complexities of a cultural process that produces such a document; not least because, as we now know, this fable fell victim to censorship. The new "Holinshed" was called in by the Privy Council almost as soon as it appeared in January 1587, and large sections of it dealing with the most up-to-the moment events, especially the Babington Plot, were deleted and replaced with a briefer and more neutral account.[18] In this unusually careful revision, largely carried out by Abraham Fleming, a second, different fable significantly survived.

A few pages later, the chronicler had paused to moralize on the Babington plot and its consequences, and, marking the spot with another marginal gloss ("A prettie apolog allusorie to the present case of malcontents") proceeded to rewrite for the occasion the ancient Aesopian fable of *The Frogs Desiring a King*:

> God make prince and people of one mind, and plant in all subjects a reverend regard of obedience and contentment of present estate, supported with justice and religion: least longing after novelties, it fare with them as with the frogs, who living at libertie in lakes and ponds, would needs (as misliking their present intercommunitie of life) with one consent sue to Jupiter for a king, and so did. Whereat he woondering,

granted their desires, and cast them an huge trunk of a tree, which besides that it made a great noise in the water as it fell, to their terrifieng; so it was cumbersome by taking up their accustomed passage: insomuch that discontented therewithall, they assaulted Jupiter with a fresh petition, complaining that (besides diverse mislikes otherwise) the king whom he gave was but a senselesse stocke, and unworthie of obedience: wherefore it would please him to appoint them another indued with life. Whereupon Jupiter sent the herne among them, who entring into the water, devoured up the frogs one after another: insomuch that the residue, seeing their new king so ravenouslie gobling up their fellowes, lamentablie weeping besought Jupiter to deliver them from the throte of that dragon and tyrant. But he (of purpose unchangeable) made them a flat answer, that (will they nill they) the herne should rule over them. (4:922)

"Whereby we are taught," the chronicler concluded, "to be content when we are well and to make much of good queene Elizabeth, by whom we enjoie life and libertie" (2:1576). Again, the applied topical moral asserts that passive obedience to the queen is the best policy. In the uncensored text these two fables would have reverberated with each other in a most uncomfortable fashion, since the second replicates the narrative premise—sequential execution of the powerless—of The Sheep and the Butcher. In the censored version, where The Frogs Desiring a King appears in splendid literary isolation, it is more easily controlled by the concluding official platitudes.

Yet, as we shall see, both the original and the subsequent political history of this fable admitted that its own structure was too complicated for certain application. On the one hand it appears to argue for a divinely sanctioned monarchy and the required obedience of subjects, no matter how harsh the rule; on the other it implies a contractual relationship, whereby the frogs freely brought monarchy upon themselves; and although the gods may argue that they now have no more choice in the matter, once the contractual basis of sovereignty has raised its logical head it is hard to lay it down. In fact, the chronicler has made matters worse than they were in simpler versions of the fable by emphasizing the earlier, republican state of the frogs, "living at libertie in lakes and ponds" or "intercommunitie" (a word here recorded for the first time in English), and moving to petition "with one consent," an important political term implying a general will. All of this jars unnecessarily with the "libertie" that is finally said to derive from Elizabeth's rule; and even more puzzling, if one puts any pressure on the metaphor, is whether she was to be identified with King Log or King Herne.

The 1587 *Chronicles*, then, establish the terms of reference for this chapter, which will broadly survey political fabling in England during Elizabeth's reign and a little beyond. One of the first major contributions was made in Edmund Spenser's *Shepheardes Calender*, published in 1579 in the context of court factionalism— the competition for influence between Burghley, on one side, and the circle of Leicester, Walsingham, and Sir Philip Sidney on the other, who were associated with a more militant Protestantism than Elizabeth herself was prepared to countenance. In 1579 those tensions were exacerbated by the queen's proposed marriage to the French duke of Alençon, a member of the same family that the English held responsible for the St. Bartholomew's Day massacre of the Huguenots. Dedicated to Sidney, and written (though anonymously) by Leicester's secretary, the *Calender* was unlikely to be neutral on these issues; though discreet it certainly had to be, given Elizabeth's extreme antipathy to any public discussion of the match. Spenser was certainly aware of the fate of a too-outspoken critic of the queen's plans, John Stubbs, whose authorship of a pamphlet attacking the marriage had been grounds for his trial for seditious libel in October of that same year. In a notorious case of political censorship, Stubbs's pamphlet, *The Gaping Gulf*, was burned, and its author, printer, and publisher were sentenced to lose their right hands. Mysteriously, the printer, Hugh Singleton, appears to have been reprieved; only to reappear as the printer of *The Shepheardes Calender*.

Although the dominant genre of the *Calender* is, obviously, the eclogue-book on the model of Virgil's, Spenser, through E. K., apparently intended a close and interesting relationship between pastoral and Aesopian discourse. There is a frontal emphasis on fables and fabulist thought, beginning with E. K.'s "Epistle" to the reader, where we are warned that those who do not cherish the vernacular are "like to the Mole in Aesopes fable, that being blynd her selfe, would in no wise be perswaded, that any beast could see," and also "Like to the dogge in the maunger, that him selfe can eate no hay, and yet barketh at the hungry bullock, that so faine would feede."[19] The "February" eclogue contains a fable of *The Oake and the Briar*, which, as E. K. remarks, "he telleth as learned of Chaucer, but it is cleane in another kind, and rather like to Aesopes fables" (p. 426); and the "May" eclogue, in case the reader had failed to notice its relation to *The Wolf and the Kid*, is also carefully glossed as "much like to that in Aesops fables, but the Catastrophe and end is farre different" (p. 440). For good measure, E. K. inserts into the notes to "February" the remark that old men who have lost their fear of God are "lyke unto the Ape, of which is sayd in Aesops fables, that oftentimes meeting the Lyon, he was at first sore aghast and dismayed," but later lost both fear and respect (p. 427). I take this fabulist insistence to be one of Spenser's strategies for making the *Calender* speak to "the meaner sorte" as well as to a courtly audience, balancing his lyric praise of Elizabeth with a strong strain of popular protest. And indeed, in the "September" eclogue he anticipated Donne's reference to *The Dog and the Shadow*, placing it, with a self-ironizing bitterness resembling Donne's, in the mouth of a spokesman for anticlerical and social reform. "To leave the good, that I had in honde, / In hope of better, that was uncouth:" says Diggon Davy, "So lost the Dogge the fleshe in his mouth" (p. 453).

But the full-fledged fables he produced are, to put it mildly, extremely difficult to read, or at least to "apply" in the manner to which an Elizabethan schoolboy was likely to have been accustomed. In "February," Spenser probably started with Aesop's fable of *The Bush and the Aubyer*, where a woodcutter is induced by one tree to cut down its rival. In this tale of "The Oak and the Briar," however, we follow the fate of an ancient oak who is finally cut down by a "husbandman" at the urging of an upstart briar, who will ultimately suffer from the loss of shelter that the great oak had provided. Spenser's fable has therefore absorbed the tradition represented by *The Hospitable Oake* in Edward's reign, whereby great patrons or political protectors were envisaged as powerful yet vulnerable shade trees.[20] But while one of "February's" referents was plausibly Leicester's fall from influence over Elizabeth, its length and complexity of detail invoke a larger scenario. The Oak is represented in terms that would better apply to a venerable religious institution:

> The Axes edge did oft turne againe,
> As halfe unwilling to cutte the graine:
> Seemed, the sencelesse yron dyd fear,
> Or to wrong holy eld did forbeare.
> For it had bene an auncient tree,
> Sacred with many a mysteree,
> And often crost with priestes crewe,
> And often halowed with holy water dewe.
> But sike fancies weren foolerie,
> And broughten this Oake to this miserye.
> (Ll. 203–11)

Such ambivalence—half awe and half critique—is consistent with Spenser's view of the pre-Reformation church; and when the Briar finds himself without shelter, he suffers from the same weather that oppresses the poet in "January" and "December" ("The biting frost nipt his stalke dead / . . . And heaped snowe burdned him so sore / that nowe upright he can stand no more"). The reader's allegiances are, therefore, subtly shifted from one side to the other as the fable proceeds, although even the notion of a "side" seems too precise for the experience; and the result is no simple recognition of hero and villain, still less the assignment of blame to a single error (rivalry, ambition, inexperience, superstition) but a tragic fable of mixed allegiances and the misunderstanding of roles and values.

In "May," Spenser produced a version of the ancient fable of *The Wolf and the Kid*, and by substituting a fox for the adversary achieved a greater emphasis on cunning. This was appropriate to the fable's most evident goal, which was anti-Catholic satire. In one of his glosses, Spenser's mysterious commentator E. K. identifies the trinkets in the fox's basket as "the reliques and ragges of popishe superstition": and he directly asserts that the "morall of the whole tale" is "to warne the protestaunt beware, howe he geveth credit to the unfaythfyll Catholique," and cites as an example the massacre of the Huguenots, "practised of Late yeares in Fraunce by Charles the nynth." In so doing, Spenser through E. K. was also identifying the topical value of Protestant alertness at the time of the *Calender*'s publication, since at this very moment Elizabeth was considering a marriage with Charles IX's brother.

But, as with "February," today's alert reader (and probably many of Spenser's original audience) might well experience a credibility gap between this explicit moral and the complex text they face. Neither court factionalism nor Protestant fervor seem sufficiently to motivate Spenser's innovations in this fable's plot and texture. Its power resides in the remarkable development of the domestic setting and—unusual in early modern poetry—of the mother-child dyad:

> Thilke same Kidde (as I can well devise)
> Was too very foolish and unwise,
> For on a tyme in Sommer season,
> The Gate her dame, that had good reason,
> Yode forth abroade unto the greene wood,
> To brouze, or play, or what shee thought good.
> But for she had a motherly care
> Of her young sonne, and wit to beware,
> Shee set her youngling before her knee,
> That was both fresh and lovely to see,
> And full of favour, as kidde mought be:
> His Vellet head began to shoote out,
> And his wrethed hornes gan newly sprout:
> The blossomes of lust to bud did beginne,
> And spring forth ranckly under his chinne.
> My sonne (quoth she) (and with that gan weepe:
> For carefull thoughts in her heart did creepe)
> God blesse thee poore Orphane, as he mought me,
> And send thee joy of thy jollitee.
> Thy father (that word she spake with payne):
> For a sigh had nigh rent her heart in twayne)
> Thy father, had he lived this day.
> To see the braunche of his body displaie,

How would he have joyed at this sweete sight?
But ah False Fortune such joy did him spight,
And cutte of hys dayes with untimely woe,
Betraying him into the traines of hys foe.
Now I a waylfull widdowe behight,
Of my old age have this one delight,
To see thee succeede in thy fathers steade.
(Ll. 173–203)

This news, that the father of the family has already fallen prey to
the Fox, creates a genuine dramatic irony, and also connects with
that other classic tale of fatal heredity—The Wolf and the Lamb—at
least as Caxton told it.

Yet here Spenser evidently recognized, and exploited to the full,
that ambiguity resident in Aesopian tradition with respect to the
relationship between speech and power, wit and innocence, one's
sense of justice and one's sympathy for the oppressed. All the
widow's warnings against opening the door to strangers are rendered useless by the histrionic skills of the Fox, who comes to the
door disguised as a "poore pedler." It is not his trinkets that gain
him entrance, but his apparent physical distress:

A Biggen (handkerchief) he had got about his braine,
For in his headpeace he felt a sore payne.
His hinder heele was wrapt in a clout,
For with great cold he had gotte the gout,
There at the dore he cast me downe hys pack,
And layd him downe, and grones, Alack, Alack.
Ah deare Lord, and sweete Sainte Charitee,
That some good body woulde once pitie mee.
(Ll. 242–48)

He employs, in effect, the very pathos that the fable's opening
claimed in its address to the reader; and when the Kid takes pity
upon him, and opens the door to his own undoing, he is only
showing the sympathy that the fable assumes and encourages in its
audience. A false victim claims a true one; and the reader is therefore required to rethink the role of suffering as a claim to authen-
ticity—certainly a more serious approach to Protestant polemic

than the usual focus on trinkets, and possibly an insight of more than ecclesiastical pertinence.

We are looking here at a remarkable achievement, though one remarkably underacknowledged. In his first independent publication, Spenser had apparently established an original position on the Aesopian fable, one that was both unimaginable from what had preceded him and unprecedented in terms of the freedoms he took with his models. Nor did Spenser's reputation as a fabulist rest only on the *Calender*. More important as precedent, at least for John Dryden, was *Prosopopoia. Or Mother Hubberds Tale*, which appeared under similar protocols ("Base is the style, and matter meane withal") that had indicated the *Calender*'s populist thematics. This story of how the Fox and Ape conspire to take over the kingdom of beasts while the true ruler, the Lion, "sleeping lay in secret shade, / His Crowne and Scepter lying him beside, / And having doft for heate his dreadfull hide" (ll. 951–53) was loosely based on two Aesopian originals, *The Lion and the Mouse* (already developed by Henryson in terms of Scottish politics) and *The Ass in the Lion's Skin*. Together they produced an emblem of royal negligence, which permits knaves to take over the government.

Unlike the majority of Aesop's fables, this one ends well, with the Lion recalled to duty by Mercury, and the Fox and the Ape (who has been wearing the Lion's skin) captured and punished. But there is an earlier phase of the narrative which does not offer the same optimism. The Fox and the Ape have been begging, the Ape got up like a wounded veteran of the wars. They encounter a "simple husbandman" who offers the Ape the job of shepherd on his farm, with the Fox as his sheepdog. Not surprisingly, the rogues ravage the flock, eating the lambs as fast as they are born; and when the time comes that they should "render up a reckning of their travels / Unto their master" they simply flee the area. "So was the husbandman left," concludes Spenser of this episode, "to his losse" (l. 341). The effect is of two parallel fables of governance by false deputy, the first a tragedy whose tone matches those of the fables within *The Shepheardes Calender*, the second a satirical comedy; and also of two contrasting models of the lawful monarch, the good but naive husbandman, and the supreme but slothful beast of prey.[21] It was not an encouraging pair of alternatives, nor, for all the summary justice of its conclusion, a respectful representation of the Elizabethan state.[22]

But precisely because it is so expanded, at the level of detail *Mother Hubberds Tale* resists any single explanation. There are elements of the Fox's behavior when in power that would certainly have suggested the fiscally-prudent Burghley (whom Elizabeth herself called her Fox)[23] especially the charge (which we now know to have been unjust) that under "the cloke of thrift, and husbandry, / For to encrease the common treasures store" he had made himself wealthy, and the concomitant complaint that during his ministry the power of the great noble families had diminished:

> For he no count made of Nobilitie,
> Nor the wilde beasts whom armes did glorifie,
> The Realmes chiefe strength and girlond of the crowne,
> All these through fained crimes he thrust adowne,
> Or made them dwell in darknes of disgrace:
> (Ll. 1183–87)

But in the earlier phase of the fable, when the tricksters first embark on their partnership, the Fox advises practices that belonged to the bottom strata of society, and justifies them by appealing to precisely that concept of liberty that Aesopian tradition, especially when governed by the *Life* of Aesop, could itself be seen to stand for. "Thus therefore I advise," says the Fox to the Ape:

> That not to anie certaine trade or place,
> Nor anie man we should our selves applie:
> For why should he that is at libertie
> Make himselfe bond? sith then we are free borne,
> Let us all servile base subjection scorne:

Just as the appeal to pathos was transferred from the Kid to his destroyer, so here the appeal to liberty is transferred to this rapacious entrepreneur, and heard as a rationalization for further rapacity. Further, and even more skittishly, Spenser develops this specious claim in the language of sixteenth-century egalitarianism, of protest from below:

> And as we bee sonnes of the world so wide,
> Let us our fathers heritage divide,

And chalenge to our selves our portions dew
Of all the patrimonie, which a few
Now hold in hugger mugger in their hand,
And all the rest doo rob of good and land.
For now a few have all and all have nought,
Yet all be brethren ylike dearly bought:
There is no right in this partition,
Ne was it so by institution
Ordained first, ne by the law of Nature,
But that she gave like blessing to each creture
As well of worldly livelode as of life,
That there might be no difference nor strife,
Ne ought cald mine or thine.
(Ll. 129–49)

As all of Spenser's readers would have realized, this was the language by which the Puritan protest of the 1580s and 1590s was linked, at least in official propaganda, with radical social protest from the Peasants' Revolt onward. In Richard Bancroft's *Survey of the Pretended Holy Discipline*, published in 1593 as anti-Puritan propaganda, the dissenters are compared to the insurrectionists of 1381:

> We live in a worlde (you know) that crieth out: *the first institution, the first institution:* everything must be brought to the *first institution.* The wordes be good, if they be well applied. But something was amisse in the Priestes application of his text, being such a like saying amongst a multitude of rebelles, viz: *When Adam digged and Eve spanne, who was then the Gentleman.*[24]

It is impossible to determine whether the Fox's appeal to the "institution / Ordained first" was intended really to discredit this tradition of protest and so to distance Spenser from his own earlier populism, or whether it merely warns that the ancient Edenic tropes of equality were capable of being abused by racketeers. *Mother Hubberds Tale* as a whole was scarcely a prudent document. Containing hints of previous censorship, it was finally published in 1591; and unsold copies of the *Complaints,* the volume in which it appeared, were apparently called in by the authorities.[25]

Spenser's fables, then, are marked by contradictions: an insistence on the Aesopian base, but considerable independence from the model; a theoretical grasp of the Aesopian ideology, but as great an interest in how those beliefs may mislead; a strong indication (through what L'Estrange referred to as "Hints and Glances") that topical meaning is present, but an equally strong resistance to having that meaning easily decoded. The story that Spenser's fabulist practice tells has itself the structure of a fable: If you find yourself in the position of the Lamb or the Kid, you had better learn how to write, at least, like a Fox.

Working in precisely the same political context—the French marriage crisis and the struggles of the Leicester-Walsingham axis to retain any influence over Elizabeth's policy—Sir Philip Sidney also turned to Aesopian tradition, but with very different effect. His position was both more exposed and more protected than Spenser's, not only because he was Leicester's nephew, but also because he had taken it upon himself to write the queen a personal letter strongly advising against the marriage. It is generally assumed that Sidney's retreat to his country estate during 1580–81, there to write most of his pastoral romance, the *Arcadia*, was a form of political prudence, if not of actual protest; and into the center of his romance Sidney inserted a long and extremely complex neo-Aesopian fable.

The fable is presented as a song within a song within the pastoral romantic narrative frame. Its singer is Philisides, manifestly Philip Sidney's own persona, and its source, he reports, is another nonfictional person, Hubert Languet, Sidney's Huguenot friend and mentor. Some of his readers, therefore, would have expected the fable to bear some relation to the political theories of the Huguenots, who argued for a monarchy limited by a contractual relation to those (the people) who bestow on any individual the sovereign power; and also for the right of reformers or "subaltern magistrates" to depose a monarch if he breaks his contract and becomes tyrannical. Sidney's fable was, indeed, loosely based both on *The Frogs Desiring a King* and its biblical analogue, Jotham's fable of the trees; but it explores in a more complex way than either, at the level of political philosophy as regenerated by Machiavelli, the origins, sanctions, and disadvantages of monarchy as an institution.

Here, because we are dealing with political *argument*, we shall need to quote most of this long poem. Before the existence of Man, the poem claims ("Such manner time there was"), the animals all lived "freely" together:

> The beasts had sure some beastly policy;
> For nothing can endure where order nis.
> For once the lion by the lamb did lie;
> The fearful hind the leopard did kiss;
> Hurtless was tiger's paw and serpent's hiss.
>> This think I well: the beasts with courage clad
>> Like senators a harmless empire had.
>
> At which, whether the others did repine
> (For envy harb'reth most in feeblest hearts),
> Or that they all to changing did incline
> (As e'en in beasts their dams leave changing parts),
> The multitude to Jove a suit imparts,
>> With neighing, bleating, braying, and barking,
>> Roaring, and howling, for to have a king.
>>   .   .   .   .   .
>
> Jove wisely said (for wisdom wisely says):
> "O beasts, take heed what you of me desire.
> Rulers will think all things made them to please,
> And soon forget the swink due to their hire.
> But since you will, part of my heav'nly fire
>> I will you lend; the rest yourselves must give,
>> That it both seen and felt with you may live."
>
> Full glad they were, and took the naked sprite,
> Which straight the earth yclothed in his clay.
> The lion, heart; the ounce gave active might;
> The horse, good shape; the sparrow, lust to play;
> Nightingale, voice, enticing songs to say.
>> Elephant gave a perfect memory;
>> And parrot, ready tongue, that to apply.
>
> The fox gave craft; the dog gave flattery;
> Ass, patience; the mole, a working thought;
> Eagle, high look; wolf, secret cruelty;
> Monkey, sweet breath; the cow, her fair eyes brought;

The ermine, whitest skin spotted with naught;
  The sheep, mild-seeming face; climbing, the bear;
  The stag did give the harm-eschewing fear.

The hare her sleights; the cat his melancholy;
Ant, industry; and cony, skill to build;
Cranes, order; storks, appearing holy;
Chameleon, ease to change; duck, ease to yield;
Crocodile, tears which might be falsely spilled.
  Ape great thing gave, though he did mowing stand:
  The instrument of instruments, the hand.

Each beast likewise his present brings;
And (but they drad their prince they oft should want)
They all consented were to give him wings.
And ay more awe towards him for to plant,
To their own work this privilege they grant:
  That from thenceforth to all eternity
  No beast should freely speak, but only he.

Thus man was made; thus man their lord became;
Who at the first, wanting or hiding pride,
He did to beasts' best use his cunning frame,
With water drink, herbs meat, and naked hide,
And fellow-like let his dominion slide,
  Not in his sayings saying "I," but "we";
  As if he meant his lordship common be.

But when his seat so rooted he had found
That they now skilled not how from him to wend,
Then gan in guiltless earth full many a wound,
Iron to seek, which gainst itself should bend
To tear the bowels that good corn should send.
  But yet the common dam none did bemoan,
  Because (though hurt) they never heard her moan.

Then gan he factions in the beasts to breed;
Where helping weaker sort, the nobler beasts
(As tigers, leopards, bears and lion's seed)
Disdained with this, in deserts sought their rests;
Where famine ravin taught their hungry chests,

That craftily he forced them to do ill;
Which being done, he afterwards would kill

For murder done, which never erst was seen,
By those great beasts. As for the weakers' good,
He chose themselves his guarders for to been
Gainst those of might of whom in fear they stood,
As horse and dog; not great, but gentle blood.
    Blithe were the commons, cattle of the field,
    Tho when they saw their foen of greatness killed.

But they, or spent or made of slender might,
Then quickly did the meaner cattle find,
The great beams gone, the house on shoulders light;
For by and by the horse fair bits did bind;
The dog was in a collar taught his kind.
    As for the gentle birds, like case might rue
    When falcon they, and goshawk, saw in mew.

Worst fell to smaller birds, and meanest herd,
Who now his own, full like his own he used.
Yet first but wool, or feathers, off he teared;
And when they were well used to be abused,
For hungry throat their flesh with teeth he bruised;
    At length for glutton taste he did them kill;
    At last for sport their silly lives did spill.

But yet, O man, rage not beyond thy need;
Deeme it no gloire to swell in tyranny.
Thou art of blood; joy not to make things bleed.
Thou fearest death; think they are loath to die.
A plaint of guiltless hurt doth pierce the sky.
    And you, poor beasts, in patience bide your hell,
    Or know your strengths, and then you shall do well.[26]

Like the 1587 chronicler's version of *The Frogs Desiring a King*,
Sidney's fable tells how all the creatures had once enjoyed a well-
balanced "policy," which combined aspects of the biblical peaceable kingdom with those of the Roman republic ("Like senators
a harmless empire [they] had") until it occurred to them to ask
Jove for a king. Jove first warns them, as Jotham did the Israelites,

that monarchy will only lead to tyranny, and then accedes to their request, on the condition that if he provides the life principle, the creatures will all contribute their own characteristics to the new creation. The result is Man, a mixture of good and sinister qualities, which in combination give him absolute power. A part of the fable's effectiveness derives, I submit, from its subtle contest between conventions, the traditional attributes of the different species being reallocated so as to cross the normal boundaries between strong and weak, the benign and the untrustworthy. Traditionally monarchical symbols, the lion and the eagle (and, in the special case of Elizabeth, the ermine, symbol of purity) are combined with animals more often associated with courtiers (parrot, wolf, fox, and dog) or with the common people (industrious ant, perpetually victimized sheep). The ape provided the "Instrument of Instruments," the hand; and for the ultimate gift the creatures, who have previously all enjoyed "perfect speech," agree on a great sacrifice: "That from thenceforth to all eternity / No beast should freely speak, but only he."

It is hardly a surprise, then, when Jove's prediction is fulfilled and Man becomes a tyrant, driving away (like the Fox in Spenser's fable) the great wild beasts, forcing them, in desperation, to become predators and so susceptible to punishment; and turning those who are weaker into either his servants or his prey. This section of the poem is clearly represented as an allegory of class relations, and of the extent to which class warfare can be conceived as neither necessary nor perennial, but rather produced by stress emanating from the top of the political system. It is also clearly specific to the Elizabethan system. The distinction between those of "great" lineage who have been exiled and criminalized, and those of "gentle blood" who are employed to serve the state and to police their superiors is directly pertinent to Elizabeth's reliance on Burghley, and prophetic of her later struggle with the second earl of Essex. Indeed, Sidney's use of the term "factions" as the consequence of monarchical manipulation is a sardonic comment on what has been claimed as Elizabeth's greatest contribution to the pragmatics of rule, her ability to manage rival interest groups. This poem suggests that she actually fostered faction in order to maintain her own supremacy.

Instead, then, of the crude antithesis between the passivity of

King Log and the cruelty of King Stork, Sidney provided a subtle analysis of current and competing theories of monarchy, in which divinely sanctioned power (Jove's "heavenly fire") is incorporated into an anatomy of the role such as Machiavelli might have produced, had he chosen to extend his analogy of how the prince is composed of both the lion and the fox.

Sidney resolutely extended the original fable's capacity to suggest how the theory of monarchy's acceptance is dependent on two conflicting premises, divine origin and that particular version of contract theory that supposes a people, initially capable of self-government, consenting to transfer the common sovereignty to a single figure.[27] While his attitude toward the "multitude" acting as such contains a measure of aristocratic disdain,[28] his theory of commonwealth is carried not only by the utopian "beastly policy" and "harmless empire," but also by the triple appearance of "common." So long as the monarch is uncertain of his power he "fellow-like" adopts a corporate rhetoric, "Not in his sayings saying 'I,' but 'we'; / As if he meant his lordship common be" (a sardonic gloss on the so-called "royal we"). When he turns to violence, however, his first step is to violate "the common dam," the maternal earth that he shares with the animals, who in fact preceded his late arrival on or from it; and one of his primary strategies is to persuade the "commons, cattle of the field" that it is in their interest that the great wild beasts (whom he has forced into a posture of hostility to the commons) be destroyed. Behind this satire lies an intuitive and perhaps nostalgically feudal notion in which diversity of rank would not be incompatible with peaceful cooperation, and in which the weak would be protected rather than preyed on by the strong.

When the fable ends, Sidney remarks that its shepherd audience was bemused by "the strangeness of the tale . . . scanning what he should mean by it" (p. 259). Subsequent criticism has experienced the same difficulties;[29] but one obvious key to its interpretation was the textual reference back, at the close, to The Frogs Desiring a King. When recording that fable, Phaedrus had explained its original historical context—a coup d'état by Pisistratus in the mid-sixth century B.C., by which Athenian democracy, already under internal strain, was temporarily ended. At the end of his version of the

fable, Phaedrus had also explained that as Jove told the frogs to
endure the misery of the crane, so Aesop instructed the Athenians
to accept their present misfortune, lest worse befall:

> ... "Vos quoque, o cives," ait
> "hoc sustinete, maius ne veniat, malum."

Here, clearly, is the source of Sidney's final moral also: but with
a certain difference. His fable ends with a double message, addressed to a double audience:

> But yet, O man, rage not beyond thy need;
> Deem it no gloire to swell in tyranny.
>
> . . . . .
>
> And you, poor beasts, in patience bide your hell,
> Or know your strengths, and then you shall do well.

The traditional advice to the frogs to observe a stoical patience is
now qualified: first by the warning directed to the monarch; second, by that adjectival "poor," as in Caxton's version of *The Sheep and
the Butcher*, a candid direction of sympathy; and especially by that
barely explicit threat of an alternative ("Or know your strengths")
to passive obedience.

Here, then, is another kind of metafable—an overview of the
system by which human failings are emblematically recognized
in the animal kingdom and then, at a second level of translation,
perceived to be somehow intensified, mimetically actualized, in
the sphere of political action. Given the unsettled state of political
theory in Europe at the end of the sixteenth century, given Sidney's
own uneasy situation as one of Elizabeth's courtiers, it would have
been surprising to find anywhere, let alone in a courtly poem,
an unequivocal definition of an acceptable polity; but, nevertheless, the choices are distinguished with remarkable clarity, and
the political issues unmistakable. Compared to Spenser's fables,
Sidney's is direct. The difference is partly required by his subject, which is not the temporary shifts in the factional balance at
Elizabeth's court, but political theory in the abstract; but while
Spenser's response to political censorship was to create a smoke-
screen, Sidney's was to render articulate even the conditions of
the fable's telling. His choice of genre for this central poem in the

Old Arcadia is surely to be found in his insistence on the last and greatest gift that the creatures gave their king—the renunciation of their freedom of speech. Unnecessary to the fable's plot, this gesture explains why the fable itself became a necessary ingredient of Elizabethan discourse. It is deeply connected to the theory of language built into the ancient *Life* of the Father of the fable, which contains three premises: the first, that the fabulist mysteriously recovers the Adamic prerogative of differentiating (naming) the creatures; the second, that he thereby recalls a still more innocent age when beasts themselves could speak;[30] and the third, that by making them speak again as metaphors for a brutal society he emancipates his own speech, which would otherwise remain forbidden and unfree.

That actual censorship was on Sidney's mind as the *Old Arcadia* took shape seems indisputable; for another poem prior to Philisides' fable seems to address it directly (as well as recalling the late medieval bird poems, especially the anonymous *Parliament of Birds* that De Worde had printed in the 1520s, and that Kitson had reprinted in 1565).[31] In a debate as to how shepherds (poets) can educate their society, Geron ("old man") warns a younger colleague against imprudent critique of the powerful:

> Fie, man; fie, man; what words hath thy tongue lent?
>
> . . . . .
>
> We oft are angrier with the feeble fly
> For business where it pertains him not
> Than with the pois'nous toads that quiet lie.
> I pray thee what hath e'er the parrot got,
> And yet they say he talks in great men's bow'rs?
>
> . . . . .
>
> Let swan's example siker serve for thee,
> Who once all birds in sweetly singing passed,
> But now to silence turned his minstrelsy.
> For he would sing, but others were defaced:
> The peacock's pride, the pie's pilled flattery,
> Cormorant's glut, kite's spoil, kingfisher's waste,
> The falcon's fierceness, sparrow's lechery,
> The cuckoo's shame, the goose's good intent,
> E'en turtle touched he with hypocrisy.

And worse of other more; till by assent
Of all the birds, but namely those were grieved,
Of fowls there called was a parliament.
There was the swan of dignity deprived,
And statute made he never should have voice,
Since when, I think, he hath in silence lived.[32]

In January 1581, while Sidney was probably at work on his romance, the House of Lords introduced an "Act against seditious
words and rumours" (23 Eliz. Cap. II), sometimes referred to as
the "statute of silence." The measure was clearly in response to the
French marriage negotiations and Elizabeth's insistence that they
not be discussed in press or pulpit; and between this real parliament and Arcadia's fabulous one there is a more than coincidental
resemblance.

Sidney, then, looked to the Aesopian fable as a medium of comment on the *concept* of monarchy, Spenser as a medium of criticism
of its *practice*. Given that shift in political relations which, all over
early modern Europe, centralized power in single figures controlling larger geographical units than before, both were predictable responses to what some have called the age of absolutism.
Although in England monarchy was never so absolute—not subject to constitutional limitation—as was claimed at the time and
has been subsequently argued by both its supporters and opponents, there were obviously phases in the reigns of all the Tudors,
with the exception of Edward VI, when the relationship between
sovereign and subject seemed unduly weighted in favor of the
former. The period of the French marriage negotiations (1579–
81) was one such juncture, the time of the Babington plot in 1586
was evidently another. And the fable's usefulness as an increasingly complex medium of political analysis (and hence of political
resistance) is demonstrated in part (though the argument must
here remain entirely circular) by its appearance and reappearance
at moments of crisis, or at least of visible strain on the ligaments
of the social body.

But sometimes, and also at moments of strain, we can witness
the turn to fable for what seems a contrary purpose—by writers
convinced that contemporary power relations were the best they
could be. In the same year that Spenser produced *The Shepheardes*

Calender, John Lyly, notorious for his efforts to ingratiate himself with Elizabeth, produced the second instalment of his mannered novella whose protagonist Euphues gave his name to a certain kind of stylistic excess. Licensed for the press in July 1579, *Euphues and His England* offered its readers an intensely nationalistic reading experience, whereby Euphues, as a visitor to England from Greece, is treated, mostly through conversation, to an idealized survey of English life and customs. And whereas in the first instalment Lyly had peppered his text with what Sidney was later to call "unnatural natural history," similes derived from the plant and animal kingdom, in *Euphues and His England* this habit revealed its affinity with a certain kind of fabulist practice.

Euphues and His England in fact offers its readers three extended tales of the birds, the beasts, and the bees; and although only the central one is (almost) identified as a fable, all three are generically related and share the same political philosophy. And while Euphues himself introduces the first, the second and third are produced by good old Fidus of Canterbury, whose name, location, and vocation (gardener and husbandman) ostentatiously proclaim his function as a reliable narrator, the same claim that Sidney made for "old Languet" and his "old true tales." The fabulist mode is established when Fidus, offering Euphues hospitality, begins apologizing for his house; to which Euphues replies with a version of the parliament of fowls:

> When all the birds were appointed to meet, to talk of the Eagle, there was great contention at whose nest they should assemble, every one willing to have it at his owne home, one preferring the nobility of his birth, another the statelinesse of his building: . . . at last the swallow said they should come to his nest, beeing commonly of filth, which all the Birds disdaining, said: Why, thy house is nothing else but dirt. And therefore (answered the Swallow) would I have talke there of the Eagle: for being the basest, the name of an Eagle will make it the bravest.[33]

Partially hidden in this deferential statement is a reference to yet another parliament of birds ("all the birds were *appointed* to meet, to talk of the Eagle"); but "talk of the Eagle" in a parliamentary context is the last thing that Lyly intends to recommend. For Fidus embarks on the second, much longer and more complex fable by remarking that "as Kings pastimes are no playes for every one, so their secrets, their counsels, their dealings, are not to be either scanned or enquired of any way, unlesse of those that are in the like place, or serve the like person." The tale he proceeds to tell is of uncertain status. "I cannot tell," he says, "whether it bee a Canterburie tale, or a Fable in Aesope, but prettie it is, and true":

> The Foxe and the wolfe going both a filching for food, thought it best to see whether the Lion were asleepe or awake, lest bee-ing too bold, they should speed to badde. The Foxe entring into the Kings denne (a King I call the Lion) brought word to the Wolfe that hee was asleepe, and went himselfe to his owne kennell: the Wolfe desirous to search in the Lions denne, that hee might espie some fault, or steale some pray, entred boldly, whom the Lion caught in his pawes, and asked what he would? The sillie wolfe (an unapt terme for a Wolfe, yet fit, being in a Lions hands) anwered, that understanding by the Foxe, hee was a sleepe, he thought he might be at liberty to survay his lodging: unto whom the princely Lyon, with great disdaine, though little despight (for that there can be no envy in a King) said thus: Doest thou thinke that a Lion thy prince and governour can sleepe, though hee winke, or darest thou enquire whether hee winke or wake? . . . you shall both well know, and to your griefes feele, that neither the wiliness of the Foxe, nor the wildnesse of the Woolfe, ought either to see or aske, whether the Lion either sleepe or wake, bee at home or abroad, dead or alive. For this is sufficient for you to know, that there is a Lion; not, where he is, or what he doth. (Pp. 43–44)

Lyly's fable was evidently a clever variant on the Aesopian *The Lion and the Mouse*, where the moral was the lion's high-minded generosity in freeing the mouse who has dared to play on his body while he sleeps; that royal magnanimity receives its reward when the mouse later frees him from the hunter's net. But it is also clear that Lyly was alert to the satirical potential of the notorious laziness of lions between hunting periods—precisely that characteristic that Spenser turned to political critique in *Mother Hubberds Tale*. Rather than denying its zoological credit, he bypassed the question of moral responsibility and translated the problem into one of political theory. All of the monarch's doings are transferred by Lyly (in a move that James I would later insist on for himself) to the territory of *arcana imperii*, the mysterious realm of government which is beyond criticism because it is beyond secular limitation. As old Faithful moralizes his text for Euphues, it is the subject's only duty to "understand there is a king, but what he doth, is for the gods to examine, whose ordinance he is; not for men, whose overseer he is."

And then, using as a transition a condensed version of the fable of the Body (which had so vast a tradition of political use that it will require a chapter of its own), Fidus moves on to a fully structural account of the English form of government as he understands it, by way of analogy with the commonwealth of bees drawn, or so his says, from his own experience as apiarist. The classical source here was of course not Aesop, but rather Virgil, who had devoted the fourth book of his *Georgics* to beekeeping, and in an extended account of the internal regulation of the hive had provided a metaphorical compliment to Augustus, which entered the Renaissance as a paradigm of effective monarchical or imperial government.[34]

"Then how vain is it," Fidus continues, ". . . that the foot should neglect his office, to correct the face; or that subjects should seeke more to know what their Princes doe, then what they are? wherein they shew themselves as bad as beasts, and much worse then my Bees. . . ." He then proceeds to claim that the bees choose their king and direct all their endeavors to his protection:

> whom if they finde to fall, they establish again in his Throne, with no less dutie than devotion, garding him continually, as it were for fear he should miscarry, for love he should not: whom they tender with such faith and favour, that whither soever he flieth they follow him, . . . If their Prince die, they know not how to live, they languish, weepe, sigh, neither intending their worke, nor keeping their old society. And that which is moost marvellous, and almost incredible: if there be any that hath disobeied his commandments, either of purpose or unwittingly, hee killeth himselfe with his own sting,

as executioner of his owne stubbornnesse. The King himselfe hath his sting which hee useth rather for honour then punishment. (Pp. 44–45)

However implausible this may be as an empirical account of apian behavior, its message is unmistakable. Lyly seeks to produce in his readers the same internalization of loyalty, of subjection to the monarch, as that which is found (he claims) in the best of the insect communities. And if this honor community is entomologically implausible, what are we supposed to think of what follows? For here the bee-king himself supervises the means of production, and thereby provides an alternative answer to the charge of monarchical indolence:

The King himselfe not idle, goeth up and downe intreating, threatning, commanding, using the counsell of a sequell, but not losing the dignitie of a prince, preferring those that labor [to] greater authoritie, & punishing those that loiter with due severity. Al which things being much admirable, yet this is most, that they are so profitable, bring unto man both honey & waxe, each so wholesome, that we all desire it, both so necessarie that we cannot misse them. (P. 46)

In these last lines the language of natural community is particularly potent, blending as it does the novella's middle-class readership into that alluring "we all," bringing together into one "wholesome" construct authority, profit, rewards, punishments, honey, wax, needs, desires, and their gratification.

Seldom does one find so instructive an example of how, it is now often claimed, literature serves hegemony. Yet we can be reasonably sure that Lyly produced this powerful rhetorical magic as a defensive strategy, defensive against the troublesome spirits of 1579, like Spenser and Stubbs, who had taken it upon themselves to question royal policy (or perhaps, in the context of the French marriage proposal, royal desires and needs). And it is possible to detect the point at which Lyly felt defensive, to discern a slight crack in the idealizing armature where political critique might be recognized. It occurs at the point where the concept of choosing a king (the premise of Aesop's fable of the frogs) has to be given some rational, instrumental extension. "And yet," adds

Fidus, "albeit they live under a Prince, they have their privilege, and as great liberties as strait lawes":

> They call a Parliament, wherein they consult for lawes, stat-utes, penalties, chusing offices, and creating their King, not by affection, but reason: not by the greatest part, but by the better. And if such a one by chance bee chosen (for among men sometimes the worst speed best) as is bad, then is there such civill warre and dissension, that untill he be pluckt down, there can be no friendship. (P. 45)

And as Fidus's first fable had developed the theory of *arcana imperii* in a way that seems less pertinent to Elizabeth than to James I's style of government, or at least his pronouncements upon it, so the apologue of the beehive introduces into fabulous discourse the central terms of dispute between James and his parliaments—parliamentary privilege and the "great liberties" of consultation which were constantly invoked to balance royal prerogative. More surprising still, Lyly's fable actually invokes the threat of "civill warre and dissension" that James's son experienced. Lyly's ex-ample shows that even the most determined apologist might have difficulty in appropriating Aesopian tradition to the support of society's most powerful agents; but others would certainly try. In the next chapter we shall see just how prophetic *Euphues and His England* was, both of the real political developments, and of how fabulist traditions expanded to meet them.

3 ■ "The Fable Is Inverted": 1628–1700

The world is chang'd and we have Choyces,
Not by most Reasons, but most Voyces,
The Lion's trod on by the Mouse,
The lower is the upper House:

. . . . .

The feet, and lower parts, 'tis sed,
Would trample on, and off the head,
What ere they say, this is the thing,
They love the Charles, but hate the King;
To make an even Grove, one stroke
Should lift the Shrubb unto the Oake.
Anon: "A Madrigall on Justice"

I f Elizabeth's reign was, for all its strategic successes and
overall stability, occasionally vulnerable to the subversive
critical analysis that fables made possible, we would expect
the same to be even more true of the earlier seventeenth century,
when the first two Stuarts were less accomplished in maintaining
the stance defined by Lyly's Lion, of being above question. Indeed, to begin with, the fable under James continued on the track
pioneered by Spenser; as Hoyt Hudson has demonstrated, *Mother
Hubberds Tale* spawned a whole series of animal satires, with the
cast of characters extended as necessary. The earliest was Michael
Drayton's *The Owle* (1604), an extended bird polity marking the
accession of James as the Eagle. Richard Niccols produced two
such satires, the first, *The Cuckow* (1607), in obvious imitation of
Drayton's bird kingdom, the second, *The Beggers Ape*, written before 1610 but unpublished until 1617, virtually a sequel to *Mother
Hubberds Tale*. *The Cuckow* was a generalized attack on sexual loose-
ness that unfavorably contrasted Jacobean mores with Elizabeth's

ethos of chastity, and *The Beggers Ape*, which retained Spenser's Fox and Ape as the villains, was primarily directed against the sale of titles as a means of raising revenues. William Goddard's *The Owles Araygnement* (c. 1616), pointed "with some plainness" to the murder of Sir Thomas Overbury by the agents of Carr and Frances Howard; and, finally, John Hepwith's *The Calidonian Forrest*, another fable of misgovernment by false deputy (Buckingham as the Hart) extended the genre into Charles's reign. Although written at the time of Buckingham's death in 1628, Hepwith's poem was not published until 1641 when, Hudson speculates, it may have appeared in order to counter the effect of James Howell's Royalist tree-fable, *Dodona's Grove: or the Vocall Forrest*, the first instalment of which appeared in 1640.[1]

While the very existence of these neo-Spenserian texts is proof of the fable's functionality, their procedures—to attack either generalized corruption or egregious local instances of it—render them relatively inaccessible today. It was the more theoretical model provided by Sidney that would gradually emerge on the cutting edge of seventeenth-century politics. In that model, central elements of classical fables, or of the fable's history as a genre, are used as ideological principles, and against them are measured the new historical circumstances that motivated the writer to return to Aesop. For the fable to do its work in the world, a contemporary vocabulary and issues cannot merely be grafted upon a traditional matrix, but past and present must be seen to be *structurally* related. And the more people wrestled to accommodate received systems to vast social and cultural changes, the more it became evident that the fable was no rudimentary signifying system, but capable of doing advanced work in the arena of political definition.

The major issue in need of definition from Elizabeth's death to the outbreak of civil war was, in fact, peculiarly adapted to Aesopian tradition: the sanctions of royal power and its limitations, if any. In James's reign the theoretical relationship between the sovereignty vested in the king and responsibilities vested in parliament, became, of course, widely debated and contested, not least because James himself had published his views on the subject; the stock phrases that registered the contest were royal prerogative and the liberties of the subject. Parliamentary history shows a series of confrontations between king and parliament in which attempts to deal with other issues (the proposed union between England and Scotland, monopolies, impositions, the Great Contract of 1610) foundered in the impasse created by those terms; and of those confrontations, the most disruptive was the 1628–29 struggle over the Petition of Right and the resulting decision by Charles I to rule without parliament indefinitely.

In the records of the House of Commons for May 22, 1628, there appears an instance of fabulist discourse that is almost too good to be true, in its making explicit the procedure by which an old metaphor was reappropriated and reinterpreted in terms of the current crisis, and in showing how a literary training and imagination could function in political debate; not, as one might too easily assume, merely to add rhetorical force or emotive content, but to clarify and demystify an otherwise ill-defined constitutional abstraction.

The context of the discussion was whether the Petition of Right should be circumscribed by a proviso proposed by the Lords excluding the king's "sovereign power" from the terms proposed. In opposing the Lords' amendment, Sir Henry Marten (father of the regicide) spoke with unusual forcefulness and color:

> Horace dislikes the painter that *humano capiti* would join a horse's neck. Yet if he made a horse's neck alone it was good. The King may not require money but in parliament. It is a man's head; but add this clause, "unless it be by sovereign power," then it is a lion's neck, and it mars all. . . . It implies the King is trusted with a power for the destruction and also for the safety of the people. It admits also he may use "sovereign power," and if he do we may not refuse it, for it is for our protection. So it bounds up my mouth that I cannot but say that it is for the good of the people. "Sovereign power" is transcending and a high word. There is a tale in *Aesop's Fables*, the moral whereof shall be that when actions are regulated by law you may guess at the proportion, but if it be regulated by the prerogative, there is no end. The ass, the lion and the fox agreed to go on hunting, and they found good prey, and the ass was willing to make a division, and so he did laying all

into three heaps, and said to the lion, "It is your prerogative to choose." The lion took it ill and said, "It is my prerogative to choose," and he tore the ass and did eat him up. He said to the fox, "Divide you," so he took a little part of the skin, and left all the rest. The lion asked him what he meant. He answered him, "All is yours." The lion replied, "This is my prerogative," and he asked the fox who taught him that. Said he, "The calamity of the ass." [2]

The fact that this episode was recounted in four of the parliamentary journals, and in one of them with such precision, suggests a paradox: that Marten's speech was so remarkable that its textual nuances were seen as essential to the record; and that the fable he chose was so familiar that Marten could count on his audience to recognize and appreciate his divergences from it. The preexistent fabulist plot on which he depended was simple: in *The Lion, the Cow, the Goat, and the Sheep*, which usually appeared early in the Aesopian corpus, the lion and three nonpredators agree, unnaturally, to go hunting together and to divide the spoils; but when the time comes for division, the lion claims all the shares one by one, by a series of rationalizations, and none dare gainsay him. In Caxton's version, already quoted in my introduction, the lion offers a four-point claim to all four shares, culminating in naked threat: "who so ever toucheth the fourthe part he shalle be myn mortal enemy." And therefore, Caxton moralizes, "this fable techeth to al folk that the poure ought not to hold felawship with the myghty. For the myghty man is never feythfull to the poure." [3] The disparity in power relations was more emphatic in Caxton than in some other versions, where the stress fell on the fragility of the original agreement. So, for example, the reader might be admonished that reads: "Faithfulness hath been ever rare; it is more rare now-a-days: but it is and hath always been most rare among potent Men. Wherefore it is better that you live with your equals. For he that liveth with a potent man, must necessarily part ofttimes with his own right: you shall have equal dealings with your equals." [4]

The moral of Marten's version, however, is not predetermined by cultural precedent but "shall be" arrived at. The lion is bound by convention to be recognized as the king; but by retelling an ancient tale of "might makes right" in terms currently hot, especially the central and ironically repeated "prerogative," the immediately topical application is secured. The subtheme of censorship ("it bounds up my mouth that I cannot but say that it is for the good of the people") connects this fable to Sidney's in the *Arcadia*, while at the same time permitting the parliamentarian to open his mouth after all. The fox learns by the calamity of the ass to let the prerogative alone, but the fabulist learns by the example of Aesop to let the animals speak for him. And by setting his intervention in the frame of Horace's *Ars Poetica*, where the rules are established for a probable, rather than a fantastic mimesis, Marten implied that not only parliamentary debate, but the constitution itself, should be governed by the rules of a natural decorum. Men should keep their own heads on their own necks; a king who roars like a lion has become a monster.

Marten's warning, as we know, was inefficacious. In 1629 Charles's second parliament dissolved in undignified confusion, to be followed by eleven years of prerogative rule, and then by the ultimate confrontations of 1640 to 1649. The broadside ballad verses cited at the opening of this chapter show both how pervasive fabulist thinking had become, in the sense that they literally circulated on the street, and how clearly the inversion of the old fables were connected to the inversion of conventional power structures in England, in which process parliament itself is seen as the primary agent. But for a truly intelligent attempt to rethink Aesopian concepts in relation to the civil war and the republican experiment, we need to turn to John Ogilby and his *Fables of Aesop Paraphras'd in Verse*, first published in 1651 with illustrations by Francis Cleyn. Ogilby's interpretations of Aesop stand at the midpoint of both the century and the revolution, and they significantly altered the status of the fable in the second half of the century.

In Mary Pritchard's pioneering study of the political fable, Ogilby is given credit for converting the fable into a medium of historical representation. His system was signaled to the seventeenth-century reader by "politically charged" language, unmistakably referring to persons and events:

> There are, for example, several references to covenants and covenanters (Fables 3, 8, 42) and one to the "Solemn League

and Cov'nant" (32). Civil war is likewise mentioned in four fables (6, 21, 40, 72) along with a multitude of references to various kinds of rebellion. Cromwell's cavalry regiment, Ironsides, is alluded to in Fables 8 and 27, while the term "malignants," a common epithet used by the Parliamentarians to describe the Royalists, occurs in Fables 13, 17, 22, 39, 40 and 71 as both adjective and noun. Two fables, 29 and 72, mention sequestration, and four, commonweal or commonwealth (32, 47, 75 and 77). Reference is made to two issues with which Cromwell was particularly concerned during his Parliamentary career: the draining of the fens (15) and the Root and Branch bill (40, 42 and 67).[5]

This careful analysis is useful confirmation that Ogilby's *Aesop* is indeed as topical as it feels. Nor would one wish to quarrel with Pritchard's larger conclusion, that the theme of the volume as a whole is a principle of order and hierarchy, which war and rebellion subvert. But in order to substantiate my claim that Ogilby significantly altered the *status* of the fable, we need to go deeper; and one can hardly do better than begin where the seventeenth-century reader began, with the commendatory poem by William Davenant that preceded the 1651 edition.

It was certainly part of the effect intended that Davenant addressed himself to the reader "From the Tower Sep. 30. 1651," underlining the condition of many Royalists after the battle of Worcester that very month. His poem on Ogilby's paraphrases is an elegant play on ideas of imprisonment, appropriating for both politics and aesthetics the tradition of the fable as the political language of slaves, and connecting both ancient and recent styles of bondage to the freedom with which Ogilby had treated his material. Davenant begins by praising Aesop for having rescued from Egyptian priests the ancient system of hieroglyphs, by which animal symbolism conveyed knowledge of the divine, and for having restored it to "the Laitie," a challenging application of Reformation imagery to one who clearly opposed the current "reformers." He then proceeded to praise Ogilby for having performed a comparable act of rescue for Aesop:

> Blest be our Poet too! whose fire hath made
> Grave Aesop warme in Death's detested shade.

Though Verses are but Fetters deem'd by those
Who endlesse journeys make in wandring Prose,
Yet in thy Verse, methinks, I Aesop see
Less bound than when his Master made him free:
So well thou fit'st the measure of his mind,
Which, though the Slave, his body, were confind,
Seem'd, as thy wit, still unconstraind and young.
(A5v)

And he concludes with a classic defense of poetry as a form of passive resistance:

Laws doe, in vain with force our wils invade;
Since you can Conquer when you but Perswade.
(A6r)

What Davenant's poem suggested, everything that we know about Ogilby's career confirms, from his early service in Wentworth's household in Ireland, through his lost Royalist epic, the *Carolies*, to his remarkable prestige and privileges at the Restoration.[6] This was to be a Royalist collection of fables, speaking to a social and cultural elite of sudden reversals in the power relations; and to that end the classical fable was to be not only "paraphrased" but converted to a use hitherto alien to it. Instead of representing the voice of the slave or laboring class, of the disenfranchised, the powerless, the uncouth, negroid, or base, the fable is now, by the vagaries of political fortune, discovered as a vehicle of protest and solidarity for the Royalist nobility and gentry who seemed to have lost the war and had certainly, with the execution of Charles I in 1649, lost their leader. Since it was now widely understood that the only hope for the restoration of the monarchy lay in strategic acceptance of the Engagement, consolidating their position under Cromwell and waiting for the revolution to burn itself out, Ogilby's fables as a group adopted a position that was somewhere on the fine line between active and passive resistance.[7]

In accordance with this program, which required Ogilby to seem to have rightfully appropriated fabulist tradition, his fables were constructed as elegant and complex lyric structures, which nevertheless incorporated, wherever possible, the more basic strengths of earlier English fabulists. Ogilby had obviously read his

Spenser. His Fable 36, *Of the Husband-man and the Wood*, combines the original Aesopian tale—a wood foolishly provides the woodcutter with a handle for his axe—with "February's" fable of the Oak and the Briar. But taking seriously the Spenserian implications of age and rootedness, and the hints that the Oak was both person and institution, Ogilby abandoned the theme of rivalry between two trees for a far more complex narrative of political interests. For the tree with a long history he substituted an ancient forest system, "Neer a vast Comons," in which the oak is only one element:

> This wealthy grove, the Royall Cedar grac'd,
>> Whose head was fix'd among the wandring stars,
>> Above loud Meteors and the elements Wars,
> His root in th'Adamantine Center fast;
>>> This all surpast
> Crown'd Libanus; about him Elmie Peers,
> Ash, Fir, and Pine, had flourish'd many years,
> By him protected both from heat and cold.
> Eternall plants, at least ten ages old,
>> All of one mind
>> Theyr strength conjoyn'd,
>> And scorn'd the wind;
> Here highly honour'd stood the sacred Oke,
>> Whom Swains invoke,
> Which oracles, like that of Dodon, spoke.

The ancient forest, then, is clearly the English political system, in which all the trees are distinguished by their height, that is to say, their rank, from the "Comons," and in which the "Royal Cedar" (the king) is distinguished from the "sacred Oke" (the national church or its greatest representative, Archbishop William Laud). Even to name them, however, as Ogilby had no need to, detracts from the dignity that inheres naturally in the very idea of a great forest, and culturally in the concept of solidarity ("All of one mind") with which Ogilby has endowed the English aristocracy.

But the fable's point is that this defensive unity does, after all, give place to the rivalry between different types of tree that Aesop and Spenser had recognized. There is an equally clear historical ref-erent for "the under cops (that did complain / Their Soveraign / A Tyrant was)," as well as for the "rotten-hearted Elms, and Wooden

Peers," who support the husbandman's plans for chopping down some of their colleagues in order to give themselves more room. Central to the tragedy, also, is the shortsightedness of the royal cedar, who is persuaded to give the husbandman the wood he needs for a handle to his axe, thus enabling his own destruction and that of his entire kingdom—a none-too-inscrutable allusion to the Nineteen Propositions in which Charles I, many of his own supporters thought, had given away the constitutional grounds of his sovereignty; while the husbandman himself is both villain and victim, who weeps to behold "the havock his own hands had made." And if, as in Spenser's fable, the husbandman stands as he must for the monarch who mistakenly destroys something or someone of value to the land, Ogilby's husbandman must logically be the English nation itself. But the fable as a whole is, if not impersonal, honestly judicious. It offers not a narrowly partisan but a polytropic explanation of the causes of the civil war, in which there can be no simple apportionment of blame, and, because it is a tragic fable, a final moral (that kings should not put weapons into their subjects' hands) whose very inadequacy is part of the somber effect.

The tone established here is continued in another Spenserian recall, Ogilby's version of *The Wolf and the Kid*, which Spenser had adapted to the purposes of anti-Catholic propaganda. Ogilby returned in his version (*Of the She-Goat and Kid*, Fable 72) to the wolf of the Aesopian original, but the psychological details of his account, in which much is made of the goat's widowhood and her devotion to her only child, "her comfort and her care," are unmistakably derived from Spenser's "May" eclogue. They are equally unmistakably adapted to the new historical circumstances of 1651:

> A She-Goat Widowed by Civill War,
> (As many other wofull Matrons are)
> Although her sequestration a small fine
>   Had taken off,
>   Had little cause to laugh,
> For when she rose, she knew not where to dine.

"Sequestration" was a technical term employed by the Long Parliament to describe the temporary confiscation of Royalist estates, which could subsequently be released by taking the Engagement and (usually) paying a fine. Like Spenser's fable, Ogilby's dwells on the death of the kid's father at the hands of the wolf and the mother's fears for her son, whom she must leave alone to go foraging for food. But what the wolf brings to the door in 1651 is not the grab bag of religious superstition or a deceptive martyr complex, but the allure of a political loyalty that is bound to destroy its adherent. Disguising himself as "the King and Father of the Heard," the wolf addresses the kid in the language of those who had attempted to drum up military support for Charles II for the abortive campaign that ended on the field at Worcester; or, perhaps, of those who might, disguising themselves as the king's adherents, attempt to betray a trusting young man to engage in a destructive and doomed conspiracy:

> I live, whom Fame reported dead, and bring
> Good tydings, never better was the King.
> The Lyon now is fourty thousand strong,
>   Enumerous swarms,
>   Both old and young, take arms,
> And he will thunder at their Gates ere long,
> Changing their tryumph to a dolefull Song.
>   And now the Conquering Boar,
>   Of those subdu'd before,
>   Doth speedie aid implore,
> But the dissenting Brethren in one Fate,
>   Too late,
> Shall rue they turn'd this Forrest to a State.

The result, for this kid, is a situation in which all of the most sacred values of his culture are invoked to lure him to disaster: "Whom Pan, his Parents, and his King obey'd, / Duty, Belief, and Piety betraid." It is fair to ask whether Ogilby would have conceived of rendering this problem—of the psychology of loyalty in defeat—in these touching familial and adolescent terms if he had not been able to appropriate Spenser's insights, and particularly the dangers to themselves of idealism in the young; but where Spenser's message is obscure, and his effects achieved by expansive, even self-indulgent description, Ogilby's psychology is as deft as his political meaning is unavoidable.

Given the strategic compromises required by Engagement politics, Ogilby's fables also explore the psychological territory between unwise resistance and total capitulation. His version of *The Oke and the Reed* (67) somehow merges the traditional values of massive strength and ductility by suggesting the merits of postponement:

> Though strong, resist not a too potent foe;
> Madmen against a violent torrent row.
> Thou maist *hereafter* serve the Common-weale,
> Then yield till time shall better days repeale. (Italics added)

But while his own later career amply confirmed the wisdom of Ogilby's position, it was not merely a rationalization of timeserving. The ancient fable of the war between the birds and beasts, in which the bat, biologically a compromise between the warring species, decides on neutrality, now becomes in Ogilby's version (29) a traitor to *both* sides:

> The treacherous Bat was in the battell took:
> All hate the traitors look,
> > He never must display,
> > Again his wings by day,
> But hated live in some foul dustie nook,
> Cause he his Country in distresse forsook.

And the Moral points specifically to those who compounded with the new government in order to save their estates: "Or King or State their ruin they'l endure, / May they from Sequestration be secure."

Given this careful definition of the indefinable, a condition of loyal and unselfserving temporizing, we can see why Ogilby attempted to adapt to current circumstances *The Frogs Desiring a King* (12), a fable whose precedent history in the theory of political obedience had assumed a transition from a frog republic to different styles of monarchy. But because English history had, in effect, released into practice the contradictions inherent in the fable from its origins, those contradictions admitted by Holinshed's *Chronicles* and exploited by Sidney, Ogilby's version of the fable (figure 6) needed radical adjustment. It opens with the voices of the frogs,

Figure 6. John Ogilby, The Fables of Aesop Paraphrased in Verse
(London, 1668), with engravings by W. Hollar, D. Stoop, and F. Barlow.
Opposite p. 7. By permission of the British Library.

speaking from the position of whose who have once enjoyed a king but are now experiencing—and negatively—a republic:

> Since good Frogpadock Jove thou didst translate,
> How have we suffer'd turn'd into a State?
> In severall interests we divided are;
> Small hope is left well grounded peace t'obtain,
> > Unlesse again
> > Thou hear our prayer
> Great King of Kings, and we for Kings declare.

It continues with considerable wit to describe the two sovereigns, neither of whom would have suggested, in 1651, an exact political correlative.[8] First comes the log, with a huge splash:

> At last all calm and silent, in great State
> On silver billows he enthroned sate,
> Admir'd and reverenc'd by every Frog:
> His brow like fate without or frown or smile
> > Struck fear a while;
>
> . . . . .
>
> But when they saw he floated up and down,
> Unactive to establish his new Crown;
> Some of the greatest of them without dread
> Draw neerer to him; now both old and young
> > About him throng,
> > On's Crown they tread,
> And last, they play at Leap-Frog ore his head.

> Straight they proclame a fast, and all repair
> To vex Heavens King again with tedious prayer,
> This stock, this wooden Idoll to remove;
> Send them an active Prince, a Monarch stout
> > To lead them out,
> > One that did love,
> New realms to conquer, and his old improve.

The effect of this readjusted series of choices, from monarchy to republic and back again, must have been unsettling at least in 1651, where the frogs' request for the Restoration is so cynically undermined by its predetermined consequences. The Moral is emphatically not a translation of Aesop's advice to the Athenians to endure the current tyranny without complaint or resistance, but a general observation of the fickleness of the nation that assumes an objective distance from both Royalist and republican sentiment:

> No government can th'unsetled vulgar please,
> Whom change delights think quiet a disease.
> Now Anarchie and Armies they maintain,
> And wearied, are for Kings and Lords again.

But in 1665, when Ogilby reissued his *Fables*, he also added Aesop's final address to the Athenians, "To you, O Citizens, bear this, he said, / Lest you a greater mischief do invade." The referential system had in the interim become both clearer and more complicated. On the one hand, the repeated requests made to Cromwell during his Protectorate that he should assume the crown would have made it possible to identify that extremely "active Prince" as the stork; on the other, five years of experience of Charles II had already produced such considerable disillusionment with the ideal of Restoration that the frog fable took on a new lease of life. Even before the Restoration, John Milton had responded in a fury to a sermon delivered in 1656 by the Royalist divine, Matthew Griffith, which had featured *The Frogs Desiring a King* in an antipopulist argument. Milton claimed that Griffith had distorted the true meaning of the fable:

> The frogs (being once a free Nation saith the fable) petitioned Jupiter for a King: he tumbl'd among them a log. They found it insensible: they petitioned then for a King that should be active: he sent them a Crane (a Stork saith the fable) which straight fell to pecking them up. This you apply to the reproof of them who desire change: wheras indeed the true moral shews rather the folly of those, who being free seek a King; which for the most part either as a log lies heavy on his Subjects, without doing ought worthie of his dignitie and the charge to maintaine him, or as a Stork, is ever pecking them up and devouring them.[9]

When the Stuarts were reinstalled, this republican version of the fable was likely to appear in opposition poetry. Two of Marvell's verse satires assume its immediate intelligibility. One of the predictions of *Nostradamus's Prophecy* remarks of Charles II that "The Frogs shall then grow weary of their Crane / And pray to Jove to take him back againe"; and in *The Dialogue between the Two Horses*, itself formally related to the animal fable, one of the horses asks the other, "What is thy opinion of James Duke of York?" "The same that the Froggs had of Jupiters Stork," is the by now predictable answer.[10] In 1674 John Freke's ballad, *The History of Insipids*, was more outspoken still, completely abandoning the fable's classical statement of its purpose:

> Then, farewell, sacred Majesty,
> Let's pull all brutish tyrants down!
> Where men are born and still live free,
> There ev'ry head doth wear a crown.
> Mankind, like miserable frogs,
> Is wretched, kinged by storks or logs.[11]

Perhaps because *The Frogs Desiring a King* was no longer controllable, it did not appear to John Dryden a useful medium for debating the political and religious issues of 1687; at least not centrally. Yet because *The Hind and the Panther* anticipates and attempts to avert the revolution of 1688, as Milton had anticipated and attempted to avert the Restoration, Dryden does in fact allude in a single line to *The Frogs Desiring a King*, as also to the episode in 1 Samuel 8 with which, in constitutional theory, it was aligned. When the doves, in their rivalry with the chickens, summon the buzzard from abroad to be their "Potentate," and one who, Dryden's fable warns, will ultimately make them his prey, the allusion to the stork (or crane) of the classical fable is not only plausible, it is authorially encouraged; for the buzzard is, among many other alarming and reprehensible characteristics, described as "A King, whom in his wrath, th'Almighty gave."[12] Yet the warning against those who would once more disrupt the political system by displacing James II and bringing over William and Mary to restore a Protestant dynasty is, of course, only the last item in Dryden's ambitious polemical program.

In part because the poem is so argumentative, it is easy to underestimate how powerful and consistently it engages with fabulist tradition. Dryden's framing fable can be too easily forgotten as he struggles with his defense of Catholic dogma from the awkward posture of a new convert to that religion; but the fact remains that the Hind, as a nonpredatory representative of a faith now claimed as the only true one, has been chosen by Dryden to stand in for the innocent and yet highly intelligent hero of the *The Wolf and the Lamb*. Indeed, Dryden explains his move by remarking that "the Sheep and harmless Hind / Were never of the persecuting kind" (1:286–87). Against the "milk-white" Hind stands the Anglican panther, spotted by her Reformation antecedents and like them a beast of prey, yet unlike the Baptist boar, the Arian fox, or the Presbyterian wolf, potentially redeemable, "least deform'd, because reform'd the least" (1:409). Dryden thereby suggested that the fable might turn on its own history, and by means of a talking cure allow the powerless (his own tendentious image of Roman Catholicism) not merely to survive but to change the world for the better.

It is the Hind who alludes, in her debate with the Panther, both to *The Dog and the Shadow* and *The Wolf and the Lamb*, and adjusts them each to new circumstances.[13] In the first instance, the Hind complains that the Anglican compromise over the Real Presence in the Eucharist is mere wordsmanship:

> Then said the Hind, as you the matter state
> Not only Jesuits can equivocate;
> For *real*, as you now the word expound,
> From solid substance dwindles to a sound.
> Methinks an Aesop's fable you repeat,
> You know who took the shadow for the meat.
> (2:44–49)

This witty play on the relationship between physical and spiritual eating also connects fabling with equivocation, a relation which, as we shall see, Dryden himself exploited at the level of metapoetics. But sustenance connects the theological issue to the ecclesiastical, in the sense that the poem debates the respective rights of Anglicans and Roman Catholics to royal protection and preferment. With the Catholic James now on the throne, the newly Catholic poet takes the position that the Established Church is always on the verge of returning to the wolf, the Romans in England of becoming the lamb:

If *Caesar* to his own his hand extends,
Say which of yours his charity offends:
    . . . . .
When at the fountains head, as merit ought
To claim the place, you take a swilling draught,
How easie 'tis an envious eye to throw,
And tax the sheep for troubling streams below,
Or call her, (when no farther cause you find,)
An enemy profess'd of all your kind.
But then, perhaps, the wicked World wou'd think,
The *Wolf* design'd to eat as well as drink.
(3:109–10, 123–30)

There is also evidence that Dryden saturated himself in earlier English developments of the fable. In his invaluable edition of *The Hind and the Panther* and in his monograph on Dryden's poetry, Earl Miner demonstrated that the two long fables-within-a-fable that constitute most of the third part of the poem are derived from Ogilby's *Fables*. That told by the panther, the story of the martin's prophecy of disaster to the swallows, their failure to heed it, and their fatal refusal to fly south before winter, is a rewriting of Ogilby's Fable 40, *The Parliament of Birds*. That told by the hind, the story of the rivalry between the pigeons ("a sort of Doves") and the "Domestick Poultry" on an estate, echoes Ogilby's Fable 20, *Of the Doves and Hawks*, in which the doves, engaged against their will in a defensive war with the kites, call in the hawks to assist them but then become the victims of their own mercenaries. Miner showed how the essentially political premises of Ogilby's fables were adapted, by fusion with the biblical typology of dove, swallow, and cock, to Dryden's more complex subject, more complex because the politics of both church and state were involved;[14] and that in the second fable, Ogilby as model is fused with Chaucer, whose *Nun's Priest's Tale* of Chauntecleer and the Fox is used as an allegory of the dissolution of the monasteries by Henry VIII. So the Protestant pigeons berate the cock for waking them up in the morning, warning that contemporary Roman Catholics may share the fate of their imprudent forebears:

Such feats in former times had wrought the falls
Of crowing *Chanticleers* in Cloyster'd Walls.

Expell'd for this, and for their Lands they fled,
And Sister *Partlet* with her hooded head
Was hooted hence, because she would not pray a-bed.
(3:1020–25)

But Miner did not, I think, realize that a crucial passage in the
first part of the poem, which raises the problem of man's relation to the beasts, is also a rebuttal of Sidney's fable of the origins
of monarchy; crucial because, in Dryden's argument, the survival
of Catholicism in England is tied to the survival of a monarchy
without constitutional limitation.

When Dryden stands, in the first part of his poem, "like *Adam*,
naming ev'ry beast" (1:309) who will participate in his fable, he ap-
propriates to himself the role assigned to Aesop, who in 1687, the
same year as *The Hind and the Panther*, had appeared on the frontis-
piece of Francis Barlow's new and more elaborate polyglot edition
(see figure 3) as a mild and plebeian Adam surrounded by the
animals, the spokesman for a peaceable kingdom. But Dryden's
animal world is considerably more threatening; and he is careful to observe that the various beasts of the Reformed churches
are politically dangerous also. The Wolf brings with him no mark
of his kinship with "*Wickliff's* brood," "But his innate antipathy
to kings" (1:177); together with the Fox, he engages in political
sabotage abroad (the Protestant version, Dryden suggests, of Jesuit
missions, which in their own terms had been antimonarchical).
Significantly, Dryden links "Holland" (the Dutch republic) and
Scotland as hotbeds of this heresy, both "Drawn to the dreggs of a
Democracy," (1:211).

The question thus raised, about what sort of Adamic kingship
was required for this more savage kingdom, was answered in terms
readily transferable to James II. In the address "To the Reader"
that accompanied the poem in the spring of 1687, Dryden com-
plimented James on his famous or notorious "Declaration for
Liberty of Conscience," issued April 4, 1687, and part of his campaign both to extend the royal prerogative, to surround himself
with Roman Catholic appointees, and to seek the support of those
to the religious left of the established church, the Dissenters or
Nonconformists. As Dryden very well knew, this "Declaration" by
James had precisely the same unconstitutionality that had forced

his brother to withdraw a similar proclamation, similarly motivated, in 1672. Calmly finessing this issue in his preface, Dryden asserted that "some of the Dissenters in their Addresses to His Majesty have said that *He has restor'd God to his Empire over Conscience:* I Confess I dare not stretch the Figure to so great a boldness: but I may safely say, that Conscience is the Royalty and Prerogative of every Private man. He is absolute in his own Breast, and accountable to no Earthly Power, for that which passes only betwixt God and Him" (p. 120). This plan, to conceal the teeth of the prerogative by metaphorical transubstantiation, is then subtly developed in the first part of the poem, where Dryden, following Sidney, creates his image of a natural monarchy by describing Adam's creation.

> Beasts are the subjects of tyrannick sway,
> Where still the stronger on the weaker prey.
> Man onely of a softer mold is made;
> Not for his fellows ruine, but their aid:
> The noble image of the Deity.
>
> One portion of informing fire was giv'n
> To Brutes, th'inferiour family of heav'n:
>
> . . . . .
>
> But, when arriv'd at last to humane race,
> The god-head took a deep consid'ring space:
> And, to distinguish man from all the rest,
> Unlock'd the sacred treasures of his breast:
> And mercy mix'd with reason did impart;
> One to his head, the other to his heart:
> Reason to rule, but mercy to forgive:
> *The first is law, the last prerogative.*
> And like his mind his outward form appear'd;
> When issuing naked, to the wondring herd,
> He charm'd their eyes, & for they lov'd, they fear'd.
> Not arm'd with horns of arbitrary might,
> Or claws to seize their furry spoils in fight,
> Or with increase of feet t'o'ertake 'em in their flight.
> Of easie shape, and pliant ev'ry way;
> Confessing still the softness of his clay,
> *And kind as kings upon their coronation day.*
> (Ll. 245–71; italics added)

Here too, evidently, the royal prerogative is disarmed by being defined, not as individual freedom of conscience, but as the choice of an absolute monarch to set aside law when he feels compassion—a genial if somewhat disingenuous metaphor for a royal but illegal declaration of toleration. But, in addition, and in ways not apparent unless one were familiar with Sidney's fable of the origins of monarchy, Dryden here offered his own substitute for the fable of *The Frogs Desiring a King*. Unlike Sidney's first man, created as an amalgam of the divine and the bestial, this Adam matches the figure appropriated by Robert Filmer for the central arguments of the *Patriarcha*, that peculiar defense of absolute monarchy as established in Eden, published in 1680 and promoted as a tool to be used against the Whigs throughout the Exclusionist crisis. Dryden's original ruler is created solely by God, and receives no characteristics from the animals, who, in turn, make no request for a sovereign. Whereas Sidney's Jove reluctantly consented to the new creation by giving the animals "part of [his] heav'nly fire" and allowing them to finish the job, Dryden's God gave "One portion of informing fire" to the inferior creation, but created Man in "the noble image of the Deity." Nakedness and pliability are now essential characteristics, not, as in Sidney's fable, a temporary pose of vegetarian restraint. And though Dryden's fable of the origins of monarchy chooses to acknowledge the ending required by his scriptural plot (his Adam loses his innocence; "pride of Empire sour'd his balmy bloud," "the murtherer *Cain* was latent in his loins"), this transition from meekness to savagery in the ruler naturally avoids Sidney's double advice to his participants: "O man, rage not beyond thy need. . . . And you, poor beasts, in patience bide your hell, *Or know your strengths*."

But there remains the half-acknowledged problem of monarchical violence. The passage ends by casually switching fables, with a bland allusion to James as the "British Lyon" who is merciful even to his foes. The prototype of the merciful lion is, of course, the ancient fable of *The Lion and the Mouse*. In Ogilby's version of this fable the politics of monarch and subject are fully developed. The mouse, when caught, explains: "think not, great Sir, / I came to pick a hole in Royal Fur, / Nor with the Wolf and Fox did I contrive / 'Gainst you, nor question'd your Prerogative." The moral of the fable is ambiguous:

Mercy makes Princes Gods; but mildest Thrones
Are often shook with huge Rebellions:
Small Help may bring great Aid, and better far
Is Policy than Strength in Peace or War.[15]

This advice was not only descriptive of James's strategy in declaring toleration for nonconformity, but also of Dryden's strategy in *The Hind and the Panther*, designed, as the preface indicates, to persuade more of the "Sects" to withdraw themselves "from the Communion of the Panther" and join the king.

By thus representing monarchy both by Adamic kingship, as Robert Filmer had done, and by the fabulist tradition which made the lion the king of the beasts, Dryden was in fact admitting to a chasm in his own argument. As John Locke was to argue in 1689 (or indeed, if we accept Peter Laslett's argument, had *already* argued in his not yet published refutation of Filmer and support for Shaftesbury's position), the Stuart position on monarchy's origins as based on Genesis was fundamentally illogical:

> [Adam] was Created, or began to exist, by God's immediate Power, without the intervention of Parents or the preexistence of any of the same species to beget him, when it pleased God he should; and so did the Lion, the King of Beasts before him, by the same Creating Power of God: and if bare existence by that Power, and in that way, will give Dominion, without any more ado, our Author, by this Argument, will make the Lion have as good a Title to it as he, and certainly the Ancienter.[16]

And if conceived as a lion, James or any other sovereign was immediately resituated on the other side of the ethical line Dryden is attempting to draw, along with the Panther and the other beasts of prey.

It was for this reason, I suggest, that at the opening of part 3 of his poem Dryden identified yet another important model in the adaptation of Aesopian tradition:

> Much malice mingl'd with a little wit
> Perhaps may censure this mysterious writ,
>
> . . . . .
>
> Let Aesop answer, who has set to view,

Such beasts as Greece and Phrygia never knew;
And mother Hubbard in her homely dress,
Has sharply blam'd a British Lioness,
That Queen, whose feast the factious rabble keep,
Expos'd obscenely naked and a-sleep.
Led by those great examples, may not I
The wanted organs of their words supply?[17]

Why was Spenser's *Mother Hubberds Tale* so chosen for special mention? Because, I suggest, the earlier poem offered a *structural* solution to the "king of the beasts" dilemma, with its ethical ambiguities.

First, Dryden seems to have used Spenser's authority as permission to admit that the dilemma existed. By mentioning Spenser's "blaming" of the British lioness Dryden indicated that he read it as criticism of Elizabeth (and adjusted the lion's sex accordingly). And he seems to have connected Spenser's impertinence in showing the queen "Expos'd obscenely naked and a-sleep," with the famous trick played by Aesop on his master's wife, whose nakedness was thereby displayed to the philosophical community. This genealogy connects Spenser's delinquent lioness to the various lions in the English royal dynasty, and especially to Henry VIII, "A Lyon old, obscene, and furious made by lust" (1:351), linked by the word "obscene" to Spenser's critique of Elizabeth, literally her father, and whose role in bringing about the English Reformation was a primal cause of the current religious divergences.

By having admitted the liabilities of the lion myth, Dryden was freed to maneuver, and to suggest that Spenser's satirical view was not the only possibility. Indeed, in *Absalom and Achitophel* he had already introduced James as a noble lion, though that image was discolored by being put in the mouth of Shaftesbury, as part of his temptation of Monmouth, the king's illegitimate son, to lead a popular rebellion. There, Absalom advises violence to prevent violence:

Then the next Heir, a Prince, Severe and Wise,
Already looks on you with Jealous Eyes;
Sees through the thin Disguises of your Arts,
And markes your Progress in the Peoples Hearts.

Though now his mighty Soul its Grief contains;
He meditates Revenge who least Complains,
And like a Lyon, Slumbring in the way,
Or Sleep dissembling, while he waits his Prey,
His fearless Foes within his Distance draws;
Constrains his Roaring, and Contracts his Paws;
Till at the last, his time for Fury found,
He shoots with suddain Vengeance from the Ground:
The Prostrate Vulgar, passes o'r, and Spares;
But with a Lordly Rage, his Hunters teares.
(Ll. 441–54)[18]

In 1681 James had not yet properly succeeded to leonine status. In 1687, as the "British Lyon" who reappears in Dryden's bestiary, he is not only awake and alert but also merciful, pacific, a creature of courage and integrity, and legitimately king. But because of his species it is impossible to separate him absolutely from earlier members of the dynasty. Just at the moment when Dryden makes explicit his identification of the Lion with James II he carefully represents him as a figure of power under rational control, thereby admitting (by denying) the savage potential of the fabulist metaphor:

So when the gen'rous Lyon has in sight
His equal match, he rouses for the fight;
But when his foe lyes prostrate on the plain,
He sheathes his paws, uncurls his angry mane;
. . . . . .
So James, if great with less we may compare,
Arrests his rowling thunder-bolts in air.
(3:267–74)

But Spenser had also, in *Mother Hubberds Tale*, provided the model for an alternative metaphor for monarchy: The caring, if too incautious husbandman, owner of the sheep farm. Turning this too to the purposes of support rather than critique, Dryden makes his final representation of James the "Plain good Man" of the hind's own fable, a figure whose social status, as a landowner with three "lineal" estates, is carefully balanced by signs of humility and statements of personal attentiveness:

Another Farm he had behind his House,
Not overstock't, but barely for his use;
Wherein his poor Domestick Poultry fed,
And from his Pious Hands receiv'd their Bread.
(3:993–96)

This characterization was, of course, also modeled on that of the poor widow in Chaucer's *Nun's Priest's Tale*, the modest owner of Chauntecleer. As in Chaucer, the story and its teller gets its authority from the world of Aesopian materialism, or, as Leonardo put it in his fable of the razor, of "rustici villani." But in Dryden's adjustment, it elegantly supported his implied plea for toleration between the rival religions ("He therefore makes all Birds of ev'ry Sect / Free of his Farm, with promise to respect / Their sev'ral Kinds alike, and equally protect" (3:1244–46).

By once again inverting the fables he inherited, Dryden hoped to purge the image of monarchy of the negative inferences (tragic irresponsibility in the husbandman, reprehensible sloth in the lion) that had previously seemed so "natural." Yet precisely by reacting to Spenser and following his binary model, Dryden offered a view of the king's conduct in 1687 that was, while transparent in its sympathies, ambiguous at least in its rhetorical effect. Was the king a lion or a careful farmer, the Declaration of Indulgence an act of beneficence or an unconstitutional exertion of the prerogative? In the line of the best political fables, *The Hind and the Panther* remained, if not argumentatively, *structurally* evasive on this, the central political point.

As with the case of La Fontaine, I do not think we need to give this discovery a deconstructive edge. To do so is, I believe, to misunderstand Dryden's assertion that his poem is a "mysterious writ." In Steven Zwicker's account of Dryden's career, it is claimed that Dryden in *The Hind and the Panther* collated three kinds of "mysterious writ": his newly adopted theology, with its insistence that true religion consists of mysteries and hence requires one central and infallible interpreter; the indeterminacy of reference with which all language is infected; and the fable genre itself. Zwicker suggested that ambiguity was part of Dryden's subject and his special contribution; and that, therefore, the resistance of the interpolated bird fables to interpretation, and in particular the apparent confusion between William III and Gilbert Burnet as alternative prototypes for the buzzard, was fully intentional, part of Dryden's chosen disguise, a way of speaking his mind without being fully held to account.[19] It is not clear to me why being thought to refer *both* to William and Burnet was a form of personal insurance against career damage; and although it is certain that Dryden in this poem was fascinated by problems of interpretation in Scripture, and in the technical meaning of "equivocation" as saying something, under pressure, other than what one truly believes, the poststructuralist notion of the indeterminacy of language in general is not a useful interpretive tool here. As in Bellosta's account of La Fontaine and his interest in the *Life* of Aesop, a belief in the indeterminacy of language in general works against, rather than strengthening, the fable's claim to indeterminacy. A text that withholds its full meaning because of the sociopolitical constraints against open discussion is a text committed to referentiality; this does not prevent it from advertising its writerly mystery. As Hegel put the paradox, *because* the fabulist "dare not speak his teaching openly," he can "only make it intelligible in a kind of riddle which is at the same time always being solved."

But we cannot leave Dryden and the fable in 1687. For in 1700 he marked the turn of the century by producing a volume of *Fables Ancient and Modern* that contained, as its only fable in the strict sense, a new version of Chaucer's *Nun's Priest's Tale*, already, I have argued, a bulwark against the political implications of the fable as Lydgate would recover them. In his *Preface* to *Fables*, Dryden, who had read his Chaucer in editions that included the *Plowman's Tale*, noted, in order to dispose of it, the mistaken tradition of Chaucer's political radicalism: "In *Richard's* Time, I doubt, he was a little dipt in the Rebellion of the Commons; and being Brother-in-Law to *John of Ghant*, it is no wonder if he follow'd the Fortunes of that Family; and was well with Henry the Fourth when he had depos'd his Predecessor. Neither is it to be admir'd . . . if that great Politician should be pleas'd to have the greatest Wit of those Times in his Interests, and to be the Trumpet of his Praises." The effect is to make any supposed democratic sympathies disappear into the territory of patronage and political self-interest.

As Steven Zwicker defined the tone of *Fables*, its method is "not primarily figural or historical," and its context is "not political crisis" as it had been for *The Hind and the Panther*, "but poetry and eternity," "literary self-consciousness," "the sense of place and tradition in literary terms."[20] Just so. The *Preface* establishes Chaucer as "the Father of English Poetry" (replacing, we might add, Aesop as the Father of the fable), and conceives of poetry in terms of lineage and property inheritance, significantly by primogeniture: "for we have our Lineal Descents and Clans, as well as other Families: *Spencer* more than once insinuates, that the Soul of *Chaucer* was transfus'd into his Body; and that he was begotten by him Two hundred years after his Decease." And by translating the *Nun's Priest's Tale* into early modern idiom, therefore, as he claimed, preserving it for posterity, Dryden located himself in the same lineage.

Nevertheless, Dryden took this solemn occasion as an opportunity to *rewrite* Chaucer in more than linguistic terms. Consider, for instance, his description of Chauntecleer's sexual prowess. Where Chaucer had merely written that:

> This gentil cok hadde in his governaunce
> Sevene hennes for to doon al his plesaunce,
> Whiche were his sustres and his paramours,
> (Ll. 2863–65)

Dryden expatiates on the very problem of lineage that his *Preface* renders literary but his era had seen as the center of political controversy:

> This gentle Cock for solace of his Life,
> Six Misses had beside his lawful Wife;
> Scandal that spares no King, tho' ne'er so good,
> Says, they were all of his own Flesh and Blood:
> His Sisters both by Sire, and Mother's side,
> And sure their likeness show'd them near ally'd.
> But make the worst, the Monarch did no more,
> Than all the *Ptolomeys* had done before:
> When Incest is for Int'rest of a Nation,
> 'Tis made no Sin by Holy Dispensation.
> Some Lines have been maintain'd by this alone,
> Which by their common Ugliness are known.
> (Ll. 55–66)

If this passage recalls the witty opening of *Absalom and Achitophel*, in which Charles II's sexual promiscuity is given an ironic dispensation from disapproval by scriptural precedent, it also glances nastily at the fact that William III's father married his first cousin Mary, daughter of Charles I. And the rest of the poem gradually reveals that, for Dryden, it has become an allegory not of ecclesiastical but of political history. In Chauntecleer's tale of how a man dreamed his own murder, where Chaucer wrote, "the peple out sterte" (l. 3043), Dryden substituted, "The Mob came roaring out" (l. 276); and into a second tale, of how an equally prophetic dream of shipwreck was disregarded, Dryden inserted the following passage of mockery:

> Dreams are but Interludes, which Fancy makes,
> When Monarch-Reason sleeps, this Mimick wakes:
> Compounds a Medley of disjointed Things,
> A Mob of Coblers, and a Court of Kings:
> (Ll. 325–29)

These seemingly petty alterations collate with Dryden's treatment of the brief Chaucerian allusion to the Peasants' Revolt, which is carefully brought up to date. Where Chaucer wrote, in describing the barnyard clamor that follows Chauntecleer's seizure, "The dokes cryden as men wolde hem quelle" (l. 4580) Dryden substituted: "The Ducks that heard the Proclamation cry'd, / And fear'd a Persecution might betide" (ll. 736–37). And where Chaucer made a negative comparison between this uproar and "Jakke Straw and his meynee," whose uprising he had designated mere occupational rivalry ("Whan that they wolden any Flemyng kille"), Dryden ventured his own opinion that popular protest is itself a form of persecution:

> Jack Straw at London-stone with all his Rout
> Struck not the City with so loud a Shout;
> Not when with English Hate they did pursue
> A French Man, or an unbelieving Jew.
> (Ll. 742–45)

Finally, Dryden's Fox is presented, as Chaucer's certainly was not, as the protagonist in an act of sedition. Having made the same mistake as his victim, and opened his mouth incautiously, thereby losing his prey, this Reynard reveals himself as a would-be king-napper:

> Th'appearance is against me, I confess,
> Who seemingly have put you in Distress:
> You, if your Goodness does not plead my Cause,
> May think I broke all hospitable Laws,
> To bear you from your Palace-Yard by Might,
> And put your noble Person in a Fright:
>
> . . . . . .
>
> I practis'd it, to make you taste your Cheer,
> With double Pleasure first prepar'd by fear.
> So loyal Subjects often seize their Prince,
> Forc'd (for his Good) to seeming Violence,
> Yet mean his sacred Person not the least Offence.

A vision of the late 1640s, when Charles I was a prisoner of the army, here blends, in poetic retrospective, with the arguments of Shaftesbury as Dryden had represented them in *Absalom and Achitophel*, advising Monmouth to lead a popular rebellion:

> Commit a pleasing rape upon the crown.
> Secure his person to secure your cause:
> They who possess the prince, possess the laws.
> (Ll. 474–77)

It is fair to say that when Dryden entered the field, the need or fashion for fables was at its height. Ogilby's first collection was reissued in 1665, 1668, and 1675, and supplemented in 1668 with a new collection of *Aesopics*, written to take into account the changed political circumstances of the Restoration. Following Ogilby's lead, if not his partial independence from the fabulist canon, Francis Barlow had introduced in 1666 the first version of his polyglot edition, which combined the attraction of an illustrated Aesop, accompanied by a *Life*, with an encouragement to read the fables in a broader European context. This version and its main competitor, the translation of the fables and the *Life* by W. D., were constantly reprinted throughout the last three decades of the century. In both W. D.'s and Barlow's edition, as also in the anonymous *Aesop Explained . . . accommodated to the Lives and Manners of Men in* this present Age (1682), or *Aesop Naturaliz'd and Expos'd To the Publick View* (1697), the political implications of the text were either implicit or dormant, the translators apparently being content to draw on the market that had been created for them by Ogilby. Not so, however, with the two major translations that would follow and shape the eighteenth-century perception of fabulist discourse, the rival contributions of Sir Roger L'Estrange and Samuel Croxall, who took up positions diametrically opposite on the fable's social function, and chose those positions in relation to actual political parties.

Because L'Estrange and Croxall cannot be separated, I choose to postpone discussion of them until my last chapter, where the story of the fable's political afterlife is briefly and selectively told. The publication of Dryden's *Fables* conveniently serves to mark a real turning point, not least in its retrospective quality, reminding Dryden's readers of what had motivated fabulist activity throughout the century, but especially from its turbulent center onward. In its own turn towards *literary* history, even when, as in the prefatory discussion of lineage, the literary serves as a metaphor for the political, rather than the converse, *Fables Ancient and Modern* indeed looks forward to the demise of the Aesopian fable proper, or rather to the gradual disappearance of its strong relation to the real history of its early modern discoverers and rediscoverers.

4 ▪ Body Fables

Such Musicke is wise words with time concented;
To moderate stiffe minds, disposd to strive:
Such as that prudent Romane well invented,
What time his people into parts did rive,
Them reconcyld againe, and to their homes did drive.
—Spenser: The Faerie Queene (4:2:2)

He telleth them a tale, that there was a time when all the parts of the body made
a mutinous conspiracy against the belly, which they thought devoured the fruits of
each other's labour; they concluded that they let so unprofitable a spender starve.
In the end, to be short (for the tale is notorious, and as notorious that it was
a tale), with punishing the belly they plagued themselves. This applied by him
wrought such effect in the people, as I never read that only words brought forth
but then so sudden and so good an alteration; for upon reasonable conditions a
perfect reconcilement ensued.
—Sir Philip Sidney: Defence of Poesie

The Body and the Members, the ancient fable here reintroduced
by both Spenser and Sidney, is anomalous in the Aesopian
tradition as I have defined it, in that its own structure is
hierarchical from the top down. If the fabulous Life did its unsettling work by insisting on the fabulist's symbolic body and by permitting an emancipatory (if ultimately tragic) movement upward
from the bottom of the social hierarchy, The Belly and the Members,
when it works for Authority, summoning to its aid the entire idealist philosophical tradition, presupposes the existence and superiority of the head. Nevertheless, the Body fable was not entirely
reliable. It was not, and could not be made to be, inert. Just as it
was possible for Ogilby and L'Estrange in the civil war period and
afterward to fight for control over the Aesopian corpus, to attempt
to reclaim fabulist tradition for a group or a party whose political theory was itself hierarchical, so it was possible to subvert or

111

even challenge the Body fable in its own terms, by slight adjustments to or rearrangements of its components. This chapter is the story of some of those reappropriations; and as both Spenser's and Sidney's interest in the fable was in its political efficacy *as* language ("I never read that only words brought forth but then so sudden and so good an alteration")—in precisely that quality the fabulous *Life* of Aesop put in question—my focus will also be on how and to what extent language can be efficacious *against* the Body fable's apparently inarguable plot.

When Sidney wrote his *Defence of Poesie* in the early 1580s his primary concern was to protect what he called poetry and we call fiction from the repressive tendencies of English Protestant fundamentalists. We know from the first version of his *Arcadia* that he had a more complex model of fabulist discourse than implied by his use for defensive purposes of Menenius Agrippa's fable; but it was not, in fact, incompatible with his social theory. The encouragement to aristocratic independence and resistance to an over-authoritarian monarch which concluded Philisides' fable of the origins of monarchy excluded any notions of protest or rebellion by the underclasses. It is far less clear that Spenser's allusion carries *any* political valence. Himself, as I have shown, an extremely "prudent" fabulist in *The Shepheardes Calender*, he can be accused in this stanza from *The Faerie Queene* of no policy other than social reconciliation.

A more strictly political application of the fable had long been familiar to Englishmen well read in constitutional theory. It was to be found in John of Salisbury's *Policraticus* (1159). When in 1605 the antiquary William Camden published his *Remaines*, he retold the story of how John of Salisbury was treated to a version of *The Belly and the Members* by Pope Hadrian IV, in response to John's questioning of the Roman Church's financial exactions. As Camden remarked, "albeit it may seeme long, and to us not unlike that of Menenius Agrippa in Livie, yet give it the reading, and happly you may learne somwhat by it." Sidney gave us the short version, Camden a version of the long; and the expansive model will help us to establish a practice of reading for what will follow:

> All the members of the body conspired against the stomacke, as against the swallowing gulfe of all their labors; for

whereas the eies beheld, the eares heard, the handes labored, the feete traveled, the tongue spake, and all partes performed their functions, onely the stomacke lay ydle and consumed all. Hereuppon they joyantly agreed al to forbeare their labors, and to pine away their lasie and publike enemy. One day passed over, the second followed very tedious, but the third day was so grievous to them all, that they called a common Counsel; The eyes waxed dimme, the foote could not support the body, the armes waxed lasie, the tongue faltered, and could not lay open the matter; Therefore they all with one accord desired the advise of the Heart. There Reason layd open before them, that hee against whom they had proclaimed warres, was the cause of all this their misery: For he as their common steward, when his allowances were withdrawne, of necessitie withdrew theirs fro them, as not receiving that he might allow. Therefore it were a farre better course to supply him, than that the limbs should faint with hunger. So by the perswasion of Reason, the stomacke was served, the limbes comforted, and peace re-established. Even so it fareth with the bodies of Common-weales; for albeit the Princes gather much, yet not so much for themselves, as for others: So that if they want, they cannot supply the want of others; therefore do not repine at Princes heerein, but respect the common good of the whole publike estate.[1]

Camden proffered this tale as "not unlike" the one attributed to Menenius Agrippa by Plutarch and Livy. Yet in fact there are already important divergences here from the version derived from the classical historians. In Plutarch, the occasion of the fable's telling was a popular insurrection in Rome in 494 B.C., whose primary cause was the financial oppression of the plebeians by usurers, a complaint exacerbated by the last war against the Sabines in which, when the people agreed to fight on behalf of the new republic, they had been promised better financial arrangements upon their return. This promise having been broken, the plebeians now flatly refused to defend the city against a new invasion by the Volscians. When Menenius Agrippa was sent to negotiate with them, as "one of the pleasauntest olde men, and the most acceptable to the people," the objective of his tale was to pacify the plebeians.

The Belly in his fable is identified with the Senate, and as such personified and endowed with speech, defending himself against the charge of not contributing to the corporate economy, and explaining his role as that economy's central organ: "It is true, I first receyve all meates that norishe mans bodie: but afterwardes I sent it againe to the norishement of other partes of the same."[2] As a means of political persuasion, Menenius's fable is told as a comedy; the Belly "laughed" at the folly of the rebel members; and nowhere do the classical sources suggest the near-tragic conclusion so much in evidence in John of Salisbury's text as reiterated by Camden, where the suicidal corporate starvation is only averted by a second, penitent "counsel" of the insurgents.

And while one might reasonably argue that the shift from comedy to tragicomedy enhances the fable's hegemonic potential, the different occasional structure invites in the reader a certain ambivalence. For if one's sympathies are with John of Salisbury as a critic of an overcentralized and voracious papacy, Hadrian's telling of the fable will inevitably be experienced as interested, and, by the time of Camden's Protestant and nationalist retelling, as supporting the interests of a now discredited authority. This framing procedure, which involves both subjectification—identifying the fable with a particular perspective rather than a general *on dit*—and historicizing its application, should always be taken into account when determining intention or effect.

When, for example, Sir John Hayward urgently wished to allay Elizabeth's suspicions of his motives in having published a *History of Henry IV* in 1599, and, worse, having dedicated it to her uncontrollable and too ambitious subject, the second earl of Essex, he inserted a version of the fable, as a defense of the royal prerogative to tax the subject, into an "Epistle Apologeticall" to the second edition of his book. By providing his own application of the fable to English constitutional theory, with lavish use of the first person singular, Hayward attempted to reestablish his political orthodoxy. Charged with having implied that "impositions" led to Richard II's deposition, Hayward wrote:

> Ffor my part I am of opinion, that no imposition at any time have bene, either hurtfull to a prince, or hatefull to the people, except two qualities do concurre; ffirst that it be excessive,

secondly, that it be wildly and wastfully expended . . . it stand-
eth neither with reason, nor with religion for any subject to
repine against it ffor the prince is a person of authority &
trust, to imploy the goods of the people, for their common
good: either in maintayning order among themselves, or in
repelling the enterprises of their enemies: neyther can they
possibly be preserved by their prince, if they withdraw their
owne endevour and supply. And [this doctrine] the ancient
wise men have . . . endeavoured, by a fable to make familiare.

This did not, however, prevent the second edition of his *History*
from being called in and destroyed; nor did it rescue him from
the charge of complicity in Essex's rebellion in February 1601,
for which he remained imprisoned in the Tower, apparently until
Elizabeth's death. And although the edition was destroyed, the
"Epistle Apologeticall" was carefully copied in its entirety and sur-
vives in the State papers, a fact which suggests that its textual details
were scrutinized by his prosecutors as minutely as those of the
History itself.[3]

Hayward's use of the Belly fable in 1599 and Camden's in 1605
were both Elizabethan documents, and both somewhat ambiguous. Conversely, there was no doubt at all about the intentions of
Edward Forset, whose *Comparative Discourse of the Bodies Natural and
Politique*, published in 1606, was emphatically a statement of support for the new reign of James I. The entire treatise, all one hundred pages of it, was a series of variations on the theme of *The Belly
and the Members*, explicitly adjusted to the issues of concern to the
Jacobean state, including the recent Gunpowder Plot (an excellent
excuse for recalling the rebellious members), the new theoretical emphasis on royal prerogative that James's publications had
already made a matter of public interest, the unpopularity of the
Scottish favorites, and the king's first major project upon his accession, the constitutional reunion of England and Scotland. To
this end, the doctrine of sovereignty itself was supported by an
assertion that the king rules the nation as the soul the body, the
relation between the two being "a great mistery . . . as great an
Arcanum in policie, as the soule can bee in nature"; "the favorites
of a Prince" are "resembled to the fantasies of the Soule, wherewith he spotteth and delighteth himselfe"; but, adds Forset pru-

dently, "I will refraine to presse the application farther than the well-taught Subjects will of themselves conceive"; and the vaguely human shape of the British Isle, which had also been featured in Elizabethan propaganda, was given a new emphasis:

> nay hath not the whole Iland of Britannia, being a body perfectly shaped, rounded, and bounded with an invironing sea, beene a long time thus dissevered, and disfigured by that unluckie dualitie the authour of division? untill at the last the mightie and onely wonder working hand of God, wyping away the deformitie (not by any violent cutting off, but by a moulding as it were of the two heads into one) hath restored it againe to his first right, imperiall, and most monarchial greatnesse.[4]

This blending of organicist rhetoric with a Christian imperative is especially marked in Forset's preface, where, in defense of the overall argument that "Man [is] the fittest patterne to imitate in the forming of a civill state," the actual fable of Menenius Agrippa is set out in full, side by side with a scriptural parallel. Again, it is worth noting the slight shift of tone as the classical fable is repeated, from comedy to moral indignation and spiritual injunction. Menenius Agrippa is "imployed in the appeasing and persuading of the seditious revolting commons of Rome" and did "so sensibly shew them their errour, that surceasing their malignant envy wherewith they were enraged against the rulers (whom they accounted as the idle belly that swallowed the labors of their hands) they . . . were thereupon reclaymed into their bounds of obedience" (p. 4). And, continued Forset: "The like comparison is most divinely enlarged by a much better Orator, and in a much more important poynt of the unseparable union of the members of Christ with their head, and of the necessary communion of their distinct gifts and works amongst themselves." Yet the marginal reference to 1 Corinthians 12 would, if the reader had chosen to pursue the "like comparison" to its source, have delivered a far more genuinely communal message, and one more respectful of the lower members of the Christian community, than that which Forset's treatise hammered home.

In fact, Forset shared with Hayward and Camden an important assumption—that *The Belly and the Members* functioned as a metaphor for political theory by a rather remarkable act of abstraction—by translating the essentially carnal acts of eating and digestion into a political consensus as to how and by whom the financial resources of a state (or church) should be controlled. And his treatise therefore offers an important demonstration of how closely the moral arguments for obedience to authority (whether Roman republic, the papacy, or the English monarchy) were connected to, or rather were the official euphemisms for, economic interests. The slight traces we have already seen of commercial or market concepts in Lyly's fabulist defense of Elizabethan England seem faint indeed compared with Forset's newly capitalist candor; and it is amusing to compare the allegory of the Body in the second book of Spenser's *Faerie Queene*, with its merely ethical approach to the lower bodily functions, to Forset's emphasis on "Soveraigntie in his vegetable power":

> Who seeth not, that it belongeth to the office of Soveraigntie, to provide for the nourishing and maintaining of the state with necessaries, to amplifie the dominions thereof, for profit and dignitie, to spread abroad the encrease of the people by Colonies, in the nature of generating or propagating, to cherish in the subjects an appetite of acquiring of commodities; to graunt to them places of Mart and Market for the digesting of the same unto all parts of the Realme . . . to give order for the holding and retaining of that which is become their well agreeing and naturall sustenance, and for the expelling as well of the hurtfull overcharge, as the unprofitable excrements of the weale publique. (P. 13)

This emphasis on digestion as the circulation of wealth would become, as we shall see, a central metaphor in Jacobean political thought; but the excremental dimension of Forset's metaphor is as telling as the nutritional. Reminiscent of the early episodes in the fabulous *Life* of Aesop, it does not, certainly, bespeak an Aesopian fundamentalism; on the contrary, it only partly conceals a powerfully hierarchical impulse, whose largest objective is to justify, by means of the bodily metaphors, a system marked by extreme economic difference.

So that although Forset has to admit that "in the bodie naturall the sustenance is not all caried to one side, or to one part, to the pining and beguiling of the rest," he is anxious that no one should therefore infer "any paritie or equallitie, which nature herselfe abandoneth":

> for ... doth she give (in her intentions) to some more worthie and principall than the rest, a precedence to bee chiefly provided for ... The heart though it spreadeth his arteries all over the bodie, yet hee beateth and worketh more strongly with his pulses in one place than in another. ... Why then should it be grudged at, if the nobilitie and gentry of the land ... be better stored and furnished than the meaner of the people?
> (P. 45)

Forset's pamphlet can reasonably be taken, then, as the official version of the Belly fable for the early Jacobean state. It is all the more striking, therefore, to turn to the far more famous "literary" version in Shakespeare's *Coriolanus*, and to compare that much-disputed text with Forset's unmistakable intentions. And one point of which we can be certain is that the move to abstraction or mystification, by making the digestive metaphor stand for economic relations, is reversed; for, as was long ago observed, Shakespeare altered his historical sources, of which Plutarch was by far the most important, so as to shift the Belly fable back toward its literal, bodily content. By condensing into one opening scene of popular insurrection the two quite separate risings described by Plutarch, the first occasioned by extortionate interest rates and the second by a dearth brought on by the disruption of agriculture during the war against the Volscians, Shakespeare made famine the occasion of the Belly fable's telling—and therefore made visible the essential flaw in its argument. As Philip Brockbank put it for the Arden edition, "by transposing the story Shakespeare put it under severe strain. Its claim is inept, food is clearly and literally not being distributed and the people, not the patricians, have to make do with the bran." As for the teller, the rounding out of Menenius Agrippa's character as the greatest admirer of Coriolanus undermines his historical role as an acceptable mediator between patricians and plebeians; or, as Brockbank again expressed the unease of Shakespeare's readers at this point, "his adroit and disingenuous deployment of a great and valid political parable establishes his character but subtly diminishes his wisdom."[5]

But if Shakespeare's readers have noticed both the destabilizing shift in the *occasion* for the fable and the ironizing effects of subjectification, which of course drama exaggerates, they have, by and large, resisted the consequences. The majority have believed that *Coriolanus* is an antidemocratic play, and, with Brockbank, that Shakespeare must have believed in the "great and valid political parable" whose essential meaning he ultimately reinstated, by revealing the nearly fatal consequences of allowing the popular will, institutionalized by the creation of the tribunate, to intervene in the affairs of the state.

It is clear that Shakespeare must have seen his play as a medium for the discussion of contemporary sociopolitical and socioeconomic issues. Several times in 1605 and 1606 James himself referred to the opposition leaders in the House of Commons as tribunes of the people.[6] And, more importantly for his deployment of *The Belly and the Members* in the circumstances of a food riot, the summer of 1607 saw the Midlands Rising, one of the worst agricultural protests the nation had experienced, in the sense that several counties were involved, that the rising showed all of the signs of being coordinated, and, as I shall subsequently argue, the signs also of being ideologically motivated.

The rising began in Northamptonshire, whose people had three years earlier petitioned the House of Commons to intervene against "depopulation and excessive conversion of tillage into pasture."[7] Yet it quickly ceased to be a local extension of that earlier petition, and by its rapid spread to other counties began to take on the appearance of an organized rebellion. The rioters were described as "levellers" and "diggers," not, writes David Underdown, "yet with the revolutionary connotations that the terms acquired forty years later, but it was not an unthinkably long step from levelling fences to levelling social distinctions."[8] But from the government's perspective, the chief concern was the spread of the disturbance, reaching Warwickshire and Leicestershire by late May, and even after the Northampton rising had been put down in June, spreading to Lincolnshire, Derbyshire, Worcestershire, Oxfordshire, and Bedfordshire, with the last two counties, moreover, involved in revivals of previously suppressed disturbances.[9]

On June 8 one thousand levellers who had assembled at Newton, Northamptonshire, to dig out enclosures, and who refused to disperse when this proclamation was read to them, were attacked by Sir Anthony Mildmay's soldiery, both cavalry and foot. Fifty of the protesters were killed outright, "a great many wounded, and many captured and later hanged and quartered, as exemplary punishment."[10] While enclosures were the immediate cause of the rising, food shortages, in fact or in anticipation, were also a major issue. The arable price index, it is true, reflects nothing comparable to the catastrophic crop failures of 1596, when prices of all kinds of grain were more alarming than at any time since 1317; it does, however, show a sharp rise in wheat prices in 1608, and in 1609, when wheat recovered, a corresponding rise in the price of barley, the poor man's grain.[11] But there is other evidence that in 1607 both the authorities and those whom they would restrain made a theoretical connection between enclosures and dearth, even before the signs of the latter were powerful enough to register in the national statistics. On July 24, 1607, a royal proclamation complained that "there was not so much as any necessitie of famine or dearth of corne" to excuse the offenders, thereby implying that such excuse had been voiced.[12] By the following summer, the effects of the bad 1607 harvest were fully admitted. On June 1, 1608, James addressed complaints of grain hoarding, engrossing, the export of grain, unfair pricing, quality control, and even unemployment. He appealed to justices of the peace to ensure "that the poore may bee served of Corne at convenient and charitable prices," and "that the richer sort be earnestly mooved by Christian charitie, to cause their Graine to be sold under the common prices of the Market to the poorer sort."[13] And in January 1609 another proclamation prorogued the parliament (for the fourth time, and for a further eleven months) citing the royal reasons: "forasmuch as the dearth and scarcitie of all kinde of Victuall is at present great, And if it should draw so great a concourse of people hither as the Parliament will bring, it would not onely more increase the prices of al things hereabouts (which are already very high) but also draw many Gentlemen out of their Countreys, where their hospitality will give much reliefe to their poore neighbours."[14]

We can, then, reasonably infer that when Shakespeare began work on *Coriolanus*, probably in late 1609, the issue of enclosures (with its symbolic subtext of recovering what was once "common") had merged in the public consciousness[15] with the problem of dearth and food distribution. Perhaps because of the undeniability of this topical pressure on the play, critics have been eager to deny that Shakespeare was engaging in an Aesopian critique of the English system. As early as 1710, Charles Gildon reproached Shakespeare for intending to "flatter Arbitrary Power" by representing "the Commons of Rome, as if they were the Rabble of an Irish village."[16] As late as 1964 Günter Grass defined *Coriolanus* as this "bothersome play" in which Rome's plebeians, "like London's artisans, are cowardly rats and ignorant dogs."[17] This is, of course, the view of Coriolanus himself, with which literary criticism, knowingly or not, has tended to identify. Even when, as by E. C. Pettet, the relation of the opening food protest to the Midlands Rising has been taken seriously, the result has been controlled by the tradition of Shakespeare's natural conservativism. Thus Pettet concluded that the play "reflects the natural reactions of a man of substance to a recent mob rising in his country."[18]

Yet the opening scenes of *Coriolanus* (omitted or foreshortened in nineteenth-century stage adaptations) seem now a damning indictment of socioeconomic inequality, focused as they are on the primal issue of hunger. Coriolanus himself, reporting on the opening protest against the dearth, admits, for all his contempt of the rioters, that this is their issue:

> They said they were an-hungry, sigh'd forth proverbs—
> That hunger broke stone walls; that dogs must eat;
> That meat was made for mouths; that the gods sent not
> Corn for the rich men only. With these shreds
> They vented their complainings.
> (1:1:205–8)

But well before Coriolanus appears, in the play's opening exchanges, Shakespeare allows his hungry commoners to speak for themselves. "You are all resolved," says the First Citizen, "rather to die than famish?" And the response is indeed "Resolved, resolved" (1:1:3–5).

They then proceed to discuss the political economy, not without wit, and not without considerable social perspective:

> We are accounted poor citizens, the patricians good. What authority surfeits on would relieve us. If they would yield us but the superfluity while it were wholesome, we might guess they relieved us humanely; but they think we are too dear, the leanness that afflicts us, the object of our misery, is as an inventory to particularize their abundance; our sufferance is a gain to them. Let us revenge this with our pikes ere we become rakes. For the gods know I speak this in hunger for bread, not in thirst for revenge. (1:1:14–24)

One radical insight follows another; the citizens have grasped the fact that society's moral vocabulary ("We are accounted poor citizens, the patricians good") is the ideological form of economic difference, and that the reason why food that could have been used "while it were wholesome" to relieve the famine is instead being wasted is that the patricians *need* the dearth as a physical demonstration of the reality of their own wealth. "The leanness that afflicts us . . . is *as an inventory* to particularize their abundance." Extreme indigence in others is the bottom line in the symbolic computing of personal net worth.

My analysis here is affiliated with E. P. Thompson's work in social history from below. Thompson's research into food-centered protests in the eighteenth century was designed to counter the "mob" theory of popular protest, connected as it was to a profoundly condescending view of the underclasses as essentially sub-rational; and he uncovered in the eighteenth-century food "riot" unmistakable evidence of rational planning, disciplined behavior, and, most important in his view, an appeal to a "moral economy" against unjust encroachments by market values upon earlier standards of economic justice.[19] There are problems with this last proposition, not least in the inference that popular protest is essentially conservative; but here I wish to focus on Thompson's brilliant phrase for the theory he rejects, the "spasmodic" socioeconomic theory that used to see in food-centered protests only "rebellions of the belly"; that is to say, subpolitical reactions to fluctuations in the food supply by a underclass who, in Thompson's parodic account of his opponents' position, are driven only by their guts. This phrase has a striking relation to the opening scenes of *Coriolanus*; for by condensing the two insurrections of his sources into one, Shakespeare transformed a metaphorical rebellion *against* the Belly (the original plot of *The Belly and the Members*) into a literal rebellion *of* the Belly—the hungry plebeians—against the head.

Sometime between 1607, when he became Solicitor-General, and 1612, Sir Francis Bacon wrote an essay on the subject of "Seditions and Troubles," which appears in the manuscript of a new collection of his essays that Bacon intended to dedicate to Prince Henry.[20] He had, in fact, written the dedication, but the project so conceived was aborted by the prince's death on November 6, 1612; and when the 1612 edition of the *Essays* appeared, "Of Seditions and Troubles" had vanished, not to reappear until the much later and again expanded edition of 1625. We can only speculate on the reason for its earlier suppression, and the bearing its contents may have on the Midlands Rising and even, perhaps, on the first appearance of Shakespeare's play on the stage, an event that has left no documentary trace. But, for our purposes, the most interesting passage in the *Essay* is one added in the 1625 edition, from which I now quote.

"The surest way to prevent Seditions," Bacon wrote in the near aftermath of the Midlands Rising, "is to take away the matter of them." And, following his characteristically binary method of analysis, he first divided the "matter" into two kinds, "Much poverty, and much discontentment," and then between the classes:

> And if this poverty, and broken estate, in the better sort be joined with a want and necessity in the mean people, the danger is imminent and great. For the rebellions of the belly are the worst. As for discontentments, they are in the politic body like to humours in the natural, which are apt to gather a preternatural heat and to inflame. And let no prince measure the danger of them by this whether they be just or unjust; for that were to imagine people to be too reasonable; who do often spurn at their own good.[21]

The opening sentences, here italicized, were not included in the 1607–12 version of Bacon's text. They could easily have been added as a further meditation on the "Politique Body"; or as a result of Bacon's parliamentary experiences in the first session after the Midlands Rising, where, as we shall see, the body politic was much in evidence; or, conceivably, by direct contact with the text of Shakespeare's play, which was, of course, available to be read in the Folio edition of 1623.

But what Bacon's essay shows, and most clearly in the 1625 version, is precisely that view of "rebellions of the Belly" that E. P. Thompson wished to correct and Shakespeare represented as a gross oversimplification. For instead of showing his plebeians spasmodically clapping their hands upon their bellies and acting out of ignorance against their better interests, Shakespeare shows them using their heads. They are not only familiar with other, monarchical versions of the fable, but have discredited in advance of its delivery Menenius Agrippa's "application":

> The senators of Rome are this good belly,
> And you the mutinous members: for examine
> Their counsels and their cares, digest things rightly
> Touching the weal o'th'common, you shal find
> No public benefit which you receive
> But it proceeds or comes from them to you,
> And no way from yourselves.
> (1:1:147–53)

Menenius has asserted the impossibility of any change in the system: "For the dearth, / The gods, not the patricians, make it, and / Your knees to them (not arms) must help," and advises them to think of the Senate as caring for them "like fathers" (1:1:71–73, 76). But if these are hegemony's biggest guns (protest will fail, the gods and the state are at once identical, benevolent, and impervious to change), the plebeians are undeceived. They know the difference between eternal laws and local legislation, and that the latter not only permits change but has recently enacted it to their own disadvantage: "Care for us! True, indeed. They ne'er cared for us yet. Suffer us to famish, and their storehouses crammed with grain; make edicts for usury, to support usurers; repeal daily any wholesome act established against the rich, and provide more piercing statutes daily to chain up and restrain the poor . . . and there's all the love they bear us." (1:1:80–86).

It is crucial for our history of *The Belly and the Members* to recognize that Shakespeare inserted this skeptical analysis *before* he released into his play that supposedly "great and valid political parable." Those who assume that Shakespeare's plebeians are pacified, as they were in Plutarch, by Menenius Agrippa's fable, have patently ignored the fact that they agree to listen, *provided* he does "not think to fob off our disgrace with a tale" (1:1:92–93). Even while it is in the telling, their "petition" for formal representation, as Coriolanus himself reports, is being granted by the Senate. This is proof, not of the tale's much vaunted efficacy, but of its irrelevance.

The Midlands Rising also happens to have been the occasion—indeed, manifestly the motive—for another application of a belly fable, though one that bears only the most subtle relationship to the tale in its classical form. On June 21, 1607, shortly after the Northamptonshire massacre, a clergyman named Robert Wilkinson preached a sermon "before the Lord Lieutenant of the County, and the rest of the Commissioners there assembled upon occasion of the late Rebellion and Riots in those parts." [22] And before the end of the year, he published the sermon and dedicated it to Thomas Cecil, earl of Exeter and baron Burleigh, styling himself Cecil's "late Chaplaine," and directing his admonitions equally at the "Oppression of the mighty, and Rebellion of the manie," (A3v). Wilkinson appealed to Cecil, precisely because he had been "meanes for the due execution of justice upon the rebellious, so likewise . . . to promote the cause & complaints of the expelled, half pined, and distressed poor, that they rebell no more" (A4r). And he urged "all states generally, not to grind the faces of the poore (Esa. 3) but the master to wage his servant that he may live; & the work-master so to wage the laborer, that he may live, & the land-lord not to rack, but so to rate his tenant that he may live, *not miserably*" (D2r; italics added).

Like Menenius Agrippa, Wilkinson cites the perennial fable of the Body, but with a different allocation of body parts and responsibility: "I know ye thinke it horrible, that (as in this late Rebellion) Mechanicall men are come to beard Magistrates, . . . but as it is an ill foot that kicketh at the head, and an ill hand that beateth it, so is it an ill head that wisheth the hand cut off, or diviseth a way to have fewer fingers on the hand" (C4v). Further, Wilkinson implicitly connected his own body fable to the "belly theory" of popular protest, confirming the rising's connection to experience or fears of dearth. His text for the sermon, in fact, was Matthew 4:4, "Man shall not live by bread alone," for which he produced a remarkably materialist exegesis: "That man liveth by bread, is inferred out of the very text; for even where [the apostle] saith, 'not by bread onely,' it followeth of necessitie, that amongst other meanes, yet bread for one" (C2v). "For," he continued, "the belly sayth that bread must be had, and the soule subscribeth . . . and though reason may perswade, and authoritie command, and Preachers exhort with obedience and patience to sustaine the want of bread, yet for all that, *Venter non habet aures* [the belly has no ears], in case of extreame hunger men will not be perswaded, but they will have bread" (D2v).

And as with Shakespeare's plebeians, Wilkinson also made it clear that his own revision of the Belly fable occurs in a context where the bodily hierarchies are no longer being taken for granted. The Belly may have no ears, but the rebellious members have brains enough to reason from hunger to structural social change. First, he explains, they complained "upon some just cause. . . . Afterward . . . they murmured not for want, but for wantoness. . . . But . . . their murmuring came to that, that they would change the state, . . . they would have no head at all; right as in the daies of the Judges, wherein 'there was no King in Israell, but every man did what was right in his own eyes' " (Judges 17:6). The rising was alarming, in other words, precisely because of the rational capacity of its leaders, their will to challenge the official constructions of the body politic, and to substitute for them a headless body of their own.

At least within the history of the fable, this image was more than coincidentally prophetic of what happened in the 1640s; but in order to understand how deeply, and not ornamentally, the story of Body fables coincides with the historical narrative, we need to return to the supposedly extra-literary discourse of Jacobean politics. For, not surprisingly, as Shakespeare was completing and presumably staging his play, the head was busy with fabling of its own. In the spring of 1610, when James's much prorogued parliament was finally recalled to business, the body metaphor reappears in parliament in a context that returns it to its normal functions; that is to say, with food's distribution standing metaphorically for the economic system and its rationale. Since the only reason for recalling parliament was the king's need for funds, Robert Cecil, as Treasurer, had an uncomfortable role to play, given what had occurred during the long prorogation, and perhaps contributed to its length. He chose to ask for a supply by alluding to the venerable image of incorporation: "The king (being the politic head) can receive no other good from the body of this parliament, severed in itself, than the natural head can receive comfort when there is interruption of the passages between the brain and the heart, whereof the best issue can be no other but the effects of a dead palsy which taketh away motion first and life after."[23] In Salisbury's fable the threat of organic death is used as an argument for unity of purpose between king and parliament, but with the Head, obviously, replacing the Belly as the governing organ; and on March 3 Sir Edwin Sandys, arguing for the crown, developed the request for supply in terms of the original fable's emphasis on distribution and digestion, by curiously conflating the head and the liver:

> the liver draweth nourishment before it distributeth blood to the body. The ocean must be filled by the rivers and the head maintained by the members. The sun doth not ingulf the waters nor the liver engross the blood but distributeth where it want, for natura *abhorret a vacuo*. All kings have had ordinary resort to the bounty of their subjects and the people must be as ready to return to the king as the king is ready to distribute to the people. (2:43)

On March 21 James himself circulated (in a speech that was promptly published) a version of the Body fable that was more surgical than nutritional, more threatening than reconciliatory, and more cerebral than corporate: "As for the head of the naturall body," he said: "the head hath the power of directing all the members of the body to that use which the judgement in the head thinkes most convenient. It may apply sharpe cures, or cut off corrupt members, let blood in what proportion it thinks fit, and as the body may spare."[24] Finally, in November, in a crucial conference called between representatives of both Houses, the earl of Northampton actually delivered a version of the classical fable itself.

"Some say," he began, "that the king must begin to relieve himself out of the riches of his own best means and not to depend only upon the supplies of state":

> The like quarrel was made once to the belly, as we read in the Roman histories, by all the other parts, for that it engross'd and consumed whatsoever could be gained by the providence and industry of other parts, but finding by experience that upon their envious conspiracy . . . not the belly only but the head, the feet, the arms, the legs, and every part that first began the quarrel fell into decay, they fell again to their old offices and grew very much ashamed of the mutiny.[25]

But not even this heavy dose of organicism could persuade the Commons to close their side of the Great Contract that Salisbury hoped would rationalize the national finances; especially since James in the late stages of negotiation suddenly increased his demands, confirming precisely the language of Northampton's fable ("that it engross'd and consumed whatsoever could be gained by the providence and industry of other parts").

The 1610 parliament was, therefore, unable to resolve the standoff between the king's need for funds and the growing sense in the Commons that on this point—the question of how and why the country should be taxed—all constitutional theory finally turned. It is no overstatement to say that the fiscal impasse so created led more or less directly to the Petition of Right in the Caroline parliament of 1628/9, where, we remember, Sir Henry Marten engaged in some fabulous discussion of the royal prerogative in taxation; and, as a result of the subsequent suspension of parliamentary government by Charles I, to the violent systemic changes of the 1640s.

It is a strong sign of the Belly fable's vitality, as also of its unreliability, that in the first heady months of the Long Parliament John Milton should have pounced upon it and filled it with disruptive enthusiasm. "Sir," he wrote in *Of Reformation*, "the little adoe, which me thinks I find in untacking these pleasant Sophismes, puts mee into the mood to tell you a tale ere I proceed further; and Menenius Agrippa speed us." Milton's version of the fable, however, has little in common with the classical matrix except its legendary comic tone. There is no rebellion within the fable, although its original occasion was naturally just below the surface; and the Body in question is only the body of state insofar as that is reflected by the three estates in parliament, with the king as their head. Milton's fable was, evidently, an image of the Long Parliament, and is conducted throughout in a parliamentary vocabulary:

> Upon a time the Body summon'd all the Members to meet in the Guild for the common good (as Aesops Chronicles averre many stranger Accidents) the head by right takes the first seat, and next to it a huge and monstrous Wen little lesse then the Head it selfe, growing to it by a narrower excrescency. The members amaz'd began to aske one another what hee was that took place next their cheif; none could resolve.

The term "Members" has now acquired the status of a politically specific pun; and the voracious organ is now not the Belly, whether senate or people, but a monstrous, inorganic tumor—Milton's representation of the Anglican bishops in the House of Lords:

> Whereat the Wen, though unweildy, with much adoe gets up and bespeaks the Assembly to this purpose. That as in place he was second to the head, so by due of merit; that he was to it an ornament, and strength, and of speciall neere relation, and that if the head should faile, none were fitter then himselfe to step into his place; therefore hee thought it for the honour of the Body, that such dignities and rich indowments should be decreed him, as did adorne, and set out the noblest Members. To this was answer'd, that it should be consulted.

At this point in his fable, Milton introduced a Menenius Agrippa figure of his own:

> Then was a wise and learned Philosopher sent for, that knew all the Charters, Lawes, and Tenures of the Body. On him it is impos'd by all, as cheife Committee to examine, and discusse the claime and Petition of right put in by the Wen; who soone perceiving the matter, and wondring at the boldness of such a swolne Tumor, Wilt thou (quoth he) that art but a bottle of vitious and harden'd excrements, contend with the lawfull

and free-borne members, whose certaine number is set by ancient, and unrepealable Statute? . . . What good canst thou shew by thee done to the Common-weale? . . . thou containst no good thing in thee, but a heape of hard, and loathsome uncleannes, and art to the head a foul disfigurment and burden, when I have cut thee off, and open'd thee, as by the help of these implements I will doe, all men shall see.[26]

It hardly needs pointing out how densely packed is this fable with ideological components. In terms of our current historiographical disagreements over the civil war period, it is instructive to see how readily Milton conflated the issue of church reform and antiprelatical prejudice with those constitutional beliefs which the Commons had, since James's first parliament, been gradually formulating: the liberties of the subject ("free-borne members"), the grounding of parliamentary practice in "Charters, Lawes, & Tenures" which from 1610 onward the lawyers in the Commons were continually excavating. There is some irony (presumably intentional) in allowing the Wen to lodge a "Petition of right"; more (unintended) in the statement that the number of the members was fixed by "ancient and unrepealable Statutes," since there was nothing more subject to violent alteration during the next twenty years than the composition of parliament; but the greatest irony of all was, of course, in Milton's assumption in 1641 that the Head's supremacy was unchallenged.

Or was that his assumption? It is worth noticing the seditious hypothesis attributed to the Wen: "that if the head should faile, none were fitter then himselfe to step into his place." If this language intuited what was coming, it was surely partly because of the narrative logic of the fable itself; for, by applying James's surgical metaphor to a part of the system that James himself, in his famous aphorism, "No bishop, no king," had declared organic, Milton must have been able to imagine a more decisive, capital, lobotomy. As the antipopulist popular fable put it, a few years later all the standard fabulist plots were inverted:

The world is chang'd and we have Voyces,
Not by most Reasons, but most Voyces,

. . . . .

The Lion's trod on by the Mouse,
The lower is the upper House:

. . . . .

The feet, and lower parts, 'tis sed,
Would trample on, and off the head.[27]

This premise, that the body politic could forcibly lose its head, was, of course, confirmed in January 1649, when Charles I was executed, and England shortly thereafter reconstituted as a republic.

In 1651, when John Ogilby published his first collection of *Fables*, this premise was dramatically presented in a new version of *The Belly and the Members* (47), now illustrated (figure 7) as a grotesque, decapitated body, with a head lying at its feet. Retitled for the occasion *Of the Rebellion of the Hands and Feet*, Ogilby's fable made no bones about its relation to contemporary events, and about its own monarchical preferences:

> Reason, once King in Man, Depos'd, and dead,
> The Purple Isle was rul'd without a head:
> The Stomach a devouring State swaid all,
> At which the Hands did burn, the Feet did gaule;
> Swift to shed blood, and prone to Civill stirs,
> These Members were, who now turn Levellers.[28]

We must recognize the story behind the fable, then, as beginning with the execution of the king and proceeding to an analysis of the internecine quarrels that beset the new republic. The Stomach, readily identifiable with the Long Parliament, is now itself challenged by more radical groups, specifically the Levellers, who from 1645 onward had demanded a more egalitarian agenda for the revolution and, in particular, proposed an extension of the franchise. In 1647 the Leveller Agreement of the People had presented, in effect, a new image of the body politic as substantially less hierarchical. In Ogilby's fable the Hands "with a drawn Sword," and hence clearly identifiable as the Army leaders, articulate the old themes of Aesopian tradition:

> Freeborne as you, here we demand our Right;
> Reason being vanquish'd, the proud Appetitie

Figure 7. John Ogilby, The Fables of Aesop Paraphrased in Verse. Opposite p. 114. By permission of the British Library.

> In Microcosmus must no Tyrant be,
> The idle Paunch shall work as well as we;

but if the king was executed in January 1649, two months later John Lilburne, William Walwyn, and other Leveller leaders were imprisoned, and Cromwell himself intervened militarily against their followers in the army. By the end of the year all hopes of a less hierarchical social structure had been redefined as utopian. The stage was set for Cromwell's emergence as the new Head, and Milton was one of his most determined apologists.

But in Ogilby's fable, the second stage of the rebellion is fatal:

> At last an extreme feeblenesse they felt,
> Saw all but skin, and their hard bones to melt,
> A pale Consumption Lording over all;
> At which a Counsell the faint Brethren call;
> The Stomach must be fed, which now was so
> Contracted, that like them, it answer'd, No.
> At which pale Death her cold approaches made,
> When to the dying Feet the weak Hands said,
> Brethren in evill, since we did deny
> The Bellie food, we must together die.
> All that are Members in a Common-wealth,
> Should more than Private, aim at Publick health;
> The Rich the Poor, and Poor the Rich, must aid:
> None can protect themselves with their own shade.
> But the chief cause did our destruction bring,
> Was, we Rebell'd 'gainst Reason our true King.

It seems clear that Ogilby intended to function like Spenser's "prudent Romane," reapplying "wise words with time concented" to the task of social reconciliation. And it is noticeable that while he draws on organicist theory as a model for political cooperation between classes ("The Rich the Poor, and Poor the Rich, must aid"), he avoids all of the most reprehensible nuances that the metaphor had accumulated in the early years of Stuart government.

In this entire narrative we can also see the shape of one of the most intractable questions of political theory: what, in fact, holds societies together? It is and is not a coincidence that Ogilby's Body fable appeared in 1651, in the same year as Hobbes's Leviathan. Written during and about England in the 1640s, Hobbes imagined that the problem the civil wars exemplified was unbounded human ambition, and that the solution to individual greed was the imposition of an arbitrary and unlimited sovereign power supported by military strength. Yet he chose to represent this solution as a giant body (figure 8), which clearly finessed the central issue. As restated by Foucault, the problem that emerged in political thought in the seventeenth century in England was that "of the distillation of a single will—or rather, the constitution of a unitary, singular body animated by the spirit of sovereignty—from the particular wills of a multiplicity of individuals."[29] Hobbes, however, also retained an *economic* view of the topic, one that, unlike Ogilby, he chose to express in terms of the organicist (Jacobean) metaphor of the circulation of the blood:

> By Concoction, I understand the reducing of all commodities, which are not presently consumed, but reserved for Nourishment in time to come, to some thing of equall value. . . . And this is nothing else but Gold, and Silver, and Mony . . . and the same passeth from Man to Man, within the Common-wealth; and goes round about, Nourishing (as it passeth) every part thereof; In so much as this Concoction, is as it were the Sanguinification of the Common-wealth: For naturall Bloud is in like manner made of the fruits of the Earth; and circulating, nourisheth by the way, every Member of the Body of Man.

And, like James I and his ministers, Hobbes recommends to his readers an organicist account of taxation:

> The Conduits, and Wayes by which it is conveyed to the Publique use, are of two sorts; One, that Conveyeth it to the Publique Coffers; The other, that Issueth the same out againe for publique payments. Of the first sort, are Collectors, Receivers, and Treasurers; of the second are the Treasurers againe, and the Officers appointed for payment of severall publique or private Ministers. And in this also, the Artificiall Man maintains his resemblance with the Naturall; whose Veins receiving the Bloud from the several Parts of the Body, carry it to the Heart; where being made Vitall, the Hearts by the Arteries sends it

Figure 8. Thomas Hobbes, Leviathan (London, 1651). Title page. By
permission of the Cornell University Library, Department of Rare Books.

out again, to enliven, and enable for motion all the Members of the same.[30]

Like Dryden's *Fables Ancient and Modern*, these remarkable passages look backward and forward at the same time; backward to an era in which, probably, organicist social theory was still half believed even while its traditional tropes were used with manifest policy; and forward to an era in which political theory would be increasingly dominated by economics.

In the course of his refutation of Filmer, which in turn was intended for the support of Shaftesbury and his Whig agenda, John Locke also engaged necessarily with Hobbes, who had defined the contractual spirit of society as abrogated once the sovereign power has been transferred. His *Two Treatises of Government* were begun in circumstances threatening to the Whigs, and even in 1690 published anonymously and only acknowledged as his shortly before his death—to be precise, in his will.

It is impossible to overestimate the influence of Locke's *Treatises*, the role that they played, as Peter Laslett has said, "in the growth to maturity of English liberalism, or in the development of those movements which had their issue in the American Revolution, the French Revolution and their parallels in Southern America, in Ireland, in India—everywhere where government by consent of the governed has made its impact felt."[31] In the 1990s we can, happily, add to that geographical list.

And in the *Second Treatise*, facing what those of his party regarded as the dangerous return of arbitrary government, Locke gave the Body fable its appropriate liberal turn, insisting that out of "the particular wills of a multiplicity of individuals," there can sometimes emerge, out of strong necessity, a single corporate will for change. But, insisted Locke:

> 'tis in their Legislative, that the Members of a Commonwealth are united, and combined together into a coherent living Body. This is the Soul that gives Form, Life, and Unity to the Commonwealth: From hence the several Members have the mutual Influence, Sympathy and Connexion: And therefore when the Legislative is broken, or dissolved, Dissolution and Death follows. For the Essence and Union of the Soci-

ety consists in having one Will, the Legislative, when once established by the Majority, has the declaring, and as it were keeping of that Will. (P. 426)

Astonishing statements follow: that monarchs who interfere with the legislative and electoral process are themselves to be understood not only as tyrants but rebels against the commonwealth, and that "when the Government is dissolved, the People are at liberty to provide for themselves, by erecting a new Legislative, differing from the other, by the change of Persons, or Form" (p. 429).

We can tell that Locke had fables on his mind at this point. A few pages later he dealt, ironically, with the argument that such principles are "destructive to the Peace of the World." "Who would not think it an admirable Peace betwixt the Mighty and Mean, when the Lamb, without resistance, yielded his Throat to be torn by the imperious Wolf?" (p. 435). Locke's library contained no less than six collections of fables, including Ogilby's, L'Estrange's, and *Aesop at Tunbridge*, which was published eight years after the *Two Treatises*.[32] It is not entirely clear, therefore, how we should interpret the fact that one of his last projects was the publication of an interlinear Aesop for children, thereby contributing to that misperception of the fable against which this entire project protests. Or perhaps he believed that the ancient fabulist plots were, even in simplified versions, serious business. In *Of Education*, Locke wrote: "To this purpose I think Aesop's fables the best, which being stories apt to delight and entertain a child, may yet afford useful reflections to a grown man; and if his memory retain them all his life after, he will not repent to find them there, amongst his manly thoughts and serious business."[33]

5 ■ "The World Is Chang'd": 1700–2000

When Sir Roger L'Estrange issued in 1692 his *Fables of Aesop and Other Eminent Mythologists; With Morals and Reflexions* its ideological stance would have been immediately recognizable. L'Estrange had established a reputation not only for that extreme form of theoretical royalism known as Filmerism,[1] but also as a self-appointed censor, who had lobbied successfully in 1663 for the position of Licenser of the Press, and had taken as part of his mandate not only the hunting down of unlicensed presses but also polemical writing of his own. Knighted in 1685 for helping Charles II's government to discredit the Popish Plot, he was inevitably removed from his post at William's accession in 1688, and so joined Dryden in that large group of Stuart supporters who eventually converted their second defeat into Tory party principles. But even without this knowledge of his allegiances, L'Estrange would have left the reader in no doubt as to what sociopolitical doctrine his *Aesop* was supposed to serve. For it arrived in one's hands with a massive preface setting out L'Estrange's views on the origins of the fable as a genre, and its subsequent uses in modern society.

I have already cited L'Estrange's demythologizing tendencies with respect to the *Life* of Aesop, and his desire to set aside as irrelevant "whether the Man was Streight, or Crooked, and his Name Aesop, or (as some will have it) Lochman." There was surely, as Samuel Croxall would subsequently suggest, another motive, in addition to that of the properly skeptical historian, in this attempt to distance the fable from its legendary Father and his *Life*. But for the moment I want to focus solely on what, in L'Estrange's view, the fable, irrespective of its origins, was good for. First, of course, it was good for the moral education of young children. Second, it participated in the general dignity of symbolic discourse in antiquity. "What can be said more to the Honour of This Symbolical Way of Morallizing upon Tales and Fables, then that the

Wisdome of the Ancients has been still Wrapt up in Veils and Figures" (A2r). And third, unsurprisingly, it was necessary as a vehicle of otherwise prohibited political criticism. Citing Nathan's parable to David, as a venerable bridge between sacred figures and extremely secular ones, L'Estrange proceeded to set out in his characteristically explosive style precisely those claims this book has been making all along; but giving those claims, of course, a local, anti-Whig and anti-Williamite twist:

> And what's more Ordinary, for Example, then for the most Arbitrary of Tyrants, to set up for the Advocates and Patrons of the Common Liberty; or for the most Profligate of Scoffers and Atheists, to Value themselves upon a Zeal for the Power, and Purity of the Gospels? . . . Now These People are not be dealt withal, but by a Train of Mystery and Circumlocution; a Downright Admonition looks liker the Reproach of an Enemy, than the Advice of a Friend; . . . Some People are too Proud, too Surly, too Impudent, too Incorrigible, either to Bear, or to Mend upon the Liberty of Plain Dealing. Others are too Big Again, too Vindictive, and Dangerous, for either Reproof, or Councel, in Direct Terms. They Hate any Man that's but Conscious of their Wickedness, and their Misery is like the Stone in the Bladder; There are Many Things good for't, but there's No Coming at it; and neither the Pulpit, the Stage, nor the Press, Dares so much as Touch upon't. . . . This Contrivance of Application, by Hints, and Glances, is the Only way under the Heavens to Hit it [Who shall say to a King, What Dost thou?] comes up to the very Stress of This Topique. There's no Meddling with Princes, either by Text, or Argument. Morality is not the Province of a Cabinet-Councel: And Ghostly Fathers Signify no more then Spiritual Bug-bears, in the Case of an Unaccountable Priviledge.

Further, as L'Estrange's *Fables* would continually make clear, he saw himself at a turning point in history, or perhaps, as Dryden certainly did in his *Fables*, at the end of an era. "Change of Times and Humours, calls for New Measures and Manners; and what cannot be done by the Dint of Authority, or Perswasion, in the Chappel, or the Closet, must be brought about by the Side-Wind of a Lecture from the Fields and the Forests" (A2v–B1r).

This compelling, if apoplectic, account of the hermeneutics of censorship here carries the unmistakable flavor of late seventeenth-century political culture as England returned, after the Revolution of 1688, to constitutional government, limited monarchy, and the full, if unedifying, development of political parties. The story of the fable in this environment is the story of party prejudice, which the ancient fabulist heritage marginally and occasionally ennobles. In the case of L'Estrange, it seems fair to say that that never happens, not even because L'Estrange, like Dryden, found himself disempowered by the events of 1688. His anti-Whig theory takes for granted the seeming paradox that "the Advocates and Patrons of the Common Liberty" can, to those who oppose them, themselves appear "the most Arbitrary of Tyrants." And there is an assumed parallelism between those who engineered James II's deposition and the Nonconformists, whose "Zeal for the Power, and Purity of the Gospel" can equally be seen through a hostile lens as profligacy and atheism.

And although L'Estrange also inveighs against the "Distorted Mis-Application" of the ancient fables to "Political or Personal Meanings," the "Reflexions" added to each of the fables in his collection remove all traces of the functional ambiguity to which he appeals. Where Ogilby had expanded the text of his fables so as to make them interpretive challenges, L'Estrange usually translated the briefest and most neutral version of the fable, and then pinned it down securely with an authoritarian gloss, frequently longer than the fable itself, and repeating over and over again the same political doctrine: the subject's duty of obedience, the fickleness of the mob, the dangers of giving the people the ghost of a voice in the way they shall be governed. He even managed to give a topical edge to fables that had not previously invited one. Thus *A Countryman and a Snake*, which traditionally exhibited ingratitude, now concludes with the post-1688 rhetorical question: "How many People have we read of in Story, that after a Pardon for One Rebellion, have been taken in Another with that very Pardon in their Pockets, and the Ink scarce Dry upon the Parchment?" (p. 9). And the non-canonical *A Bat, Bramble, and Cormorant*,[2] a strange fable about obsessions which speaks also about L'Estrange's own, refers to "Oliver's Enthusiastic Porter, [who] was directly Bible-Mad, and up to the Ears still in the Dark Prophets, and the Revelation" (p. 132).

L'Estrange's reading of the fable tradition was also inflected by what in his preface he referred to as "Change of Times and Humours"; that is to say, the extraordinary series of historical reversals, from Stuart monarchy to republic to Restoration and back to the Revolution of 1688, that he and his contemporaries had witnessed. This strong sense of cultural instability (which was also articulated by Dryden) lead to a version of the famous fable of *The Frogs Desiring a King*, which in L'Estrange's hands becomes an indictment of popular folly:

> This Allusion of the Frogs runs upon All Four (as they say) in the Resemblance of the Multitude, both for the Humour, the Murmur, the Importunity, and the subject Matter of the Petition, Redress of Grievances is the Question, and the Devil of it is, that the Petitioners are never to be pleas'd. In one Fit they cannot be *Without Government*: In Another they cannot bear the Yoak on't . . . One King is too Soft, and Easie for them; Another too Fierce! And then a third Change would do Better they think. Now 'tis Impossible to satisfie people that would have they know not what. They Beg and Wrangle, and Appeal, and their Answer is at last, that if they shift again, they shall be still Worse; By which, the Frogs are given to Understand the very truth of the Matter, as we find it in the World, both in the Nature, and Reason of the Thing, and in Policy, and Religion; which is, that *Kings are from God*, and that it is a Sin, a Folly, and a Madness, to struggle with his Appointments. (Pp. 20–21; italics original)

Exactly the same lesson of patience and noninterference is drawn from *The Kite, Hawk, and Pigeons*, a fable that undoubtedly reflects the influence of Dryden's interpolated fable of the rivalry between pigeons and chickens in *The Hind and the Panther*, and the summoning of the buzzard by the pigeons, to their own disaster. L'Estrange, however, was no "mysterious" writer. The topical interpretation is not to be left to chance. "This Fable," he announced, "in One Word was never more Exactly Moralized than in our Broils of Famous Memory":

> The Kite was the Evil Counsellor; The Free-Born People that Complain'd of them were the Pigeons; The Hawk was the

Power or Authority that they Appeal'd to for Protection. And what did all this come to at Last? The very Guardians that took upon them to Rescue the Pigeons from the Kite, destroy'd the Whole Dove-House, devour'd the Birds, and shar'd the Spoil among Themselves. (P. 21)

The only indeterminacy remaining is whether the "Broils of Famous Memory" were those of 1640 or 1688 or both of them simultaneously.

By the time that Samuel Croxall turned his attention to Aesop in 1722, L'Estrange's *Fables* had established themselves as the dominant version, appearing in at least eight editions between 1692 and 1720. There is no question but that Croxall's *Fables of Aesop and Others . . . With an Application to each Fable* was designed not only to compete with L'Estrange, but to discredit him as one who had distorted his classical originals, and imposed upon them a political interpretation that was not only offensive to Whigs and libertarians, but incompatible with the fable's origins. Croxall dedicated his *Fables* to George, viscount Sunbury, baron Halifax, son of the earl of Halifax, one of the chief agents of the Hanoverian (Protestant) succession, which ensured that when Queen Anne died without an heir the crown would not revert to the exiled House of Stuart. And Croxall was determined to show the connection between this modern contest, the principles of his fabulist rival, and those of the Father of the fable himself. For when receiving a legacy of such significance, he asserted we should "act, in all respects, as near as we can, to the Will and Intention of the Donor" (a7r).

Croxall's preface, therefore, entered into direct debate with L'Estrange's, beginning with the premise that the Aesopian fable was good for children. Not only was the claim pragmatically false, since no small child could possibly heft L'Estrange's monumental volume; but "what poor Devils," Croxall remarked astutely, "would L'Estrange make of those Children, who should be so unfortunate as to read his Book, and imbibe his pernicious Principles: Principles coin'd and suited to promote the Growth, and serve the Ends of Popery, and Arbitrary Power":

> Tho' we had never been told that he was Pensioner to a Popish Prince, and that he himself profess'd the same unaccountable

Religion, yet his Reflections upon Aesop would discover it to us: In every political Touch, he shews himself to be the Tool and Hireling of the Popish Faction; since, even a Slave, without some mercenary View, would not bring Arguments to justify Slavery, nor endeavour to establish Arbitrary Power upon the Basis of Right Reason. What sort of Children therefore are the blank Paper, upon which such Morality as this ought to be written? Not the Children of Britain, I hope; for they are born with free Blood in their Veins; and suck in Liberty with their very Milk. (b4r–b5r)

But Croxall was not content with having identified for the next generation (who might have forgotten or never known) the special pleading, religious agenda, and economic self-interest governing L'Estrange's interpretive stance. No less partisan himself, he nevertheless (or therefore) claimed for his own interpretation that form of validity that depends on a theory of original intention. If there had been anything in the Aesopian canon "tending to debase and inslave the Minds of Man," Croxall gibed, L'Estrange "might have pleaded that for an Excuse":

> But Aesop, tho' it was his own incidental Misfortune to be a Slave, yet pass'd the time of his Servitude among the free States of Greece; where he saw the high Esteem in which Liberty was held, and possibly learn'd to value it accordingly. He has not one Fable, or so much as a Hint, to favour L'Estrange's Insinuations; but, on the contrary, takes all Occasions to recommend a Love for Liberty, and an Abhorrence of Tyranny, and all arbitrary Proceedings. Yet L'Estrange . . . notoriously perverts both the Sense and Meaning of several Fables. (b6r)

Note that Croxall, for whom slavery was paradigmatic in terms of shaping Aesop's political consciousness, sees the material of the *Life* (about which he shares *some* of L'Estrange's skepticism) only as the tale of knowledge of difference, arrived at by deprivation. Aesop learns the value of freedom by seeing it in others, as a political ideal from which he himself is excluded. There is no theory here of the emancipatory power of wit, nor, for that matter, of that self-protective functional ambiguity which L'Estrange, in 1692 a member of a disempowered party, recognized as an enabling strategy. Croxall's position has to be based on something re-sembling the dominant Puritan hermeneutics, that the Scriptures speak plainly.

For example, Croxall suggests, we can look at the famous fable of *The Dog and the Wolf* "which Phaedrus ushers in with this Verse: *Quam dulcis sit Libertas, breviter proloquar.*" Challenged by this blunt-ness, L'Estrange had had to argue that this ancient *Libertas* "is to be understood of the Freedom of the Mind." But, wrote Croxall, in high indignation at this transcendentalizing move, "No body ever understood it so, I dare say, that knew what the other Freedom was. As for what he mentions [intellectual freedom], it is not in the Power of the greatest Tyrant that lives to deprive us of it" (b6v). Croxall's insistence on the "real" meaning of liberty as referring to the subject's rights (life, freedom from arbitrary imprisonment, and the use of his own property subject only to legal taxation) has a pragmatic force deriving more or less directly from the constitu-tional battles of the previous century. But at the same time he was, to my knowledge, the first to make fully explicit and in these same material terms the relation between Aesop's social experience and the ethos of the ancient fabulist canon. And what was thought to be true of Aesop was also, certainly, the case for Phaedrus, "whose hard Lot it had once been," Croxall reminded his readers, "to be a domestic Slave."[3]

This historical coincidence which, it is implied, led Phaedrus to become an interpreter of Aesop to his own Roman culture under the early emperors, also led directly to the construction of one of the most political fables, the one which has wound its way through these last two chapters, *The Frogs Desiring a King*. For though Phaedrus tells us that the occasion of this fable was the takeover of Athens by Pisistratus in the sixth century B.C., he himself retells it, Croxall reminds us, in another set of matching historical circumstances when his own role as mediating the tradition would scarcely have been seen as neutral:

> It is pretty extraordinary to find a fable of this Kind, furnish'd with so bold and yet polite a Turn by Phaedrus; one, who obtain'd his Freedom by the Favour of Augustus, and wrote it in the time of Tiberius; who were, successively, Usurpers of the Roman Government. If we may take his word for it, Aesop

spoke it upon this Occasion. When the Common-wealth of Athens flourish'd under good wholsom Laws of its own enacting, they relied so much upon the Security of their Liberty, that they negligently suffer'd it to run out into Licentiousness. And Factions happening to be fomented among them, by designing People, much about the same Time, Pisistratus took that opportunity to make himself Master of their Citadel and Liberties both together. The Athenians, finding themselves in a State of Slavery, tho' their Tyrant happen'd to be a very merciful one, yet could not bear the Thoughts of it; so that Aesop, when there was no better Remedy, prescribes them Patience . . . and adds, at last, *Wherefore, my Dear Countrymen, be contented with your present Condition, bad as it is, for fear a Change should be worse.* (P. 6)

A glance back at L'Estrange's treatment of this fable will demonstrate how deftly Croxall had fended off the antipopular prejudice which was part of its potential; how subtly he exploited the contemporary value of *The Frogs Desiring a King* to his own early eighteenth-century environment; and with what historical sophistication he marked the difference between the Aesopian legend and Phaedrus's redeployment of it ("if we may take his word for it") and the courage which marks or ought to mark the transmitter no less than the originator: "The Man, who, at such a Conjuncture, dar'd utter so bold a Truth, richly deserv'd his Liberty."

Croxall's *Fables* were reissued at least eighteen times in the eighteenth century, and at least ten times in the nineteenth; there were two different illustrated editions. And those of L'Estrange also continued to be republished, though somewhat less frequently, and eventually without the "Reflections." What their rivalry represented—the competition between Whigs and Tories for control over a powerful medium of political representation—was not, however, necessarily restricted to the elaborate systems Croxall and L'Estrange had developed and continued to dominate— the full-scale scale reinterpretation of fabulist tradition.[4] For there also developed at the turn of the seventeenth century what Mary Pritchard designated the Grub Street *Aesops*, a pamphlet war which began between pro- and anti-Williamite writers, but which had considerable extension into the eighteenth century, as each new ministry created a new set of political targets.

Pritchard connected this development to an unusual collection of seemingly disparate causes: the failure of parliament in 1695 to renew the Licensing Act (thereby releasing a more exorbitant strain of journalism); the Triennial Act of 1698, which ensured that political propagandists could get regular employment; the interest generated in Aesop by the scholarly dispute between Richard Bentley and Sir William Temple (a spin-off from the Phalaris controversy) as to whether Aesop was in truth the Father of the fable; and by the influence of Boursault's *Esope à la cour*, which, as adapted by Sir John Vanbrugh to the English stage, represented Aesop as a fashionable Restoration courtier.[5] "Aesop" began to appear as a character not only at court, but at the modish watering places in England and, as the focus of satire shifted to foreign policy, all over Europe. So, for example, *Aesop at Court, or, State Fables* (London, 1702) opens with an address to William in the last year of his life ("Permit old Aesop to approach thy Throne"), and develops into a virulent anti-Tory satire, including an entire fable devoted to "The Lion's Treaty of Partition," that is to say, an attack on France, which bears only a titular relation to the ancient fable of *The Lion, the Cow, the Goat, and the Sheep* of which Henry Marten had made such precise use in the parliament of 1628.

On the other hand, *Aesop the Wanderer*, published two weeks after the Battle of Blenheim, contains among its satires an elaborate revision of the fable of the great oak whose fall had interested Spenser and Ogilby; and giving the fable yet another, international twist, the author transformed the tree into a metaphor for the "tyranny" of Louis XIV over Europe in the War of the Spanish Succession:

> A Lofty Oak, the Lord of all the Field,
> Whome Boreas Winter Gusts had often try'd,
> Stood still unshaken, scorning e'er to yield,
> Spreading his Leafy Arms vast distance wide;
> Up to Jove's Pallaces towr'd his Head,
> (Assigned Dominion from his very Birth)
> O'er Thousand Acres did project his shade,
> Nor suffer'd Phoebus-Beams to kiss the fainting Earth:

Of which a Village-Swain
  Did oft complain,
And said it was not to be born,
  That he shou'd stretch so far
  His monstrous Boughs, to mar
  The Growing of his corn.[6]

This lyric-descriptive mode, itself reminiscent of Ogilby, permits the Grand Alliance initiated by William before his death to be represented in innocent pastoral terms—a combination of local rustics, who, however, are powerless against "the impenitrable Root" until "Jove from a distant Village sent a Swain" (Marlborough), and in the last stanza the pastoral is converted into a military epic:

The British Hero all the World extolls,
By whom the Empire stands, the Tyrant falls.
(P. 11)

It scarcely needs saying that in a few years Marlborough himself would become the target of fables aimed from the other direction.

As late as 1831, in the context of Grey's battle for electoral reform, his opponents could still be found invoking, at a vast conceptual distance, *The Frogs Desiring a King*. For the Badger, representing Grey himself, is reported as addressing "the assembled throng," that is to say, drumming up popular support for constitutional change, as follows:

ills by Nature ne'er were sent—
They all arise from Parliament:
(For beasts then had a constitution,
And Lions threatened dissolution.)
True, it has stood the test of time,
And therefore 'tis not in its prime;
Change the whole system of election—
Further, the world needs no correction.
Reform but this, and in a trice
The world becomes a paradise.[7]

This irony at the expense of utopian political thought is remarkably deft, if scarcely just; and it leads, not surprisingly, to a non-theoretical violent denouement in which the Badger is put down, not by political argument, but by the British Bull Dog.

No doubt some of my readers will at this stage be asking why, when so much attention has been paid to writers of whom they have never heard, nothing has been said of John Gay's *Fables*, which appeared in two collections, the first, in 1727, dedicated to the "young prince" William, duke of Cumberland, and the second published posthumously in 1738. The fact is that Gay's *Fables*, despite the description of the second volume as "mostly on Subjects of a graver and more political Turn," represent a reclamation of the genre from occasional political satire or partisan debate for what appears to be a transparent and indeed crystalline moralism of the most general kind, as appropriate, perhaps, for the instruction and amusement of an adolescent member of the royal family. Yet such a program, if reclamation it was, would not have been incompatible with Gay's production in 1628 of *The Beggar's Opera*, an extremely successful if indirect attack on Thomas Walpole and the corruptions of his Whig administration. For however intelligently writers like Ogilby and L'Estrange had attempted to wrest the political fable away from their opponents and make it serve a conservative cause, the resistance in the material base of some of the most famous fables remained visible. Another course was to write new fables altogether, or to pretend that the political history of the genre had never existed. Gay did both. In the nineteenth century the second route may also be detected in the extreme simplification of the fabulist tradition for the use of children; and whereas L'Estrange and Ogilby had fought over what "the children of Britain" should be taught by birds and beasts and their modern interpreters, the Victorians produced *The Baby's Own Aesop*, or *Aesop's Fables in Words of One Syllable*.

Yet the visible presence of ideology also survived, later and more naked than one would have imagined. In 1866 G. F. Townsend published *The Fables of Aesop, with New Applications, Morals, etc.* The need for new applications was clear, since this was the time of agitation for the Second Reform Bill, to be passed in 1867. If in the 1640s the anonymous "Madrigall on Justice" had reason if not justice to complain: "The world is chang'd and we have Choyces, / Not by more Reasons, but most Voyces," in 1866 the issues of the day were unmistakably once again those of political representation, the extension of the franchise, crowd control, the privileges of the few versus the needs of the many, and the economic differences that underlay all these. Townsend therefore calmly appropriated Croxall's translation of Aesop, while making it clear in his "Applications" that Croxall and what he represented were the unnamed phantoms against which this compilation (though without stating its purpose) was mustered. So in his commentary on *The Ox and the Frog*, the applicator reads a lesson on the inexorable law of inequality:

> If it be true that the poor shall never cease out of the land, then is poverty to be considered as a divine institution, and a subordination of rank to rank is established as the law impressed on human society by its Divine Author. Suppose it, indeed, to be possible that all could be equal on the one day, on the morrow there would be an inequality, as men had improved or abused the inheritance intrusted to them.[8]

Not surprisingly, Townsend felt it necessary to provide his own contemporary gloss on the fable of which we have seen so much, *The Frogs Desiring a King*. He began by recalling Croxall's account of the fable's occasion. Thus the statement that the Athenians finding themselves "in a State of Slavery, tho' their Tyrant happen'd to be a very merciful one, . . . could not bear the Thoughts of it" becomes "Although Peisistratus was a just and equitable ruler, the Athenian citizens bore the yoke of his government with much impatience, and entered into frequent plots and cabals for its overthrow." And he proceeded to draw a contrast between those foolish Athenians and "the people of this happy country" who are "remarkable for their loyal attachment to their sovereign." "This fable," Townsend concluded, "will be ever popular among them": "It inculcates lessons of loyalty, and fosters that spirit of obedience so dear to the hearts of Englishmen. At the same time, it teaches that it is better to bear with some defects in a mild and gentle government, rather than to seek a remedy in rash innovations or uncalled-for changes, which may result in greater evils."[9]

As for *The Body and the Members*, it too was reactivated by Townsend, in response to the tensions of nineteenth-century socioeconomic relations. As compared to the similar debates and disturbances of 1609/10, or the civil war period, or the early 1830s, a new and for some especially disturbing factor was the alliance formed between the Radical group in parliament headed by John Bright and Richard Cobden and the embryonic trade union movement, the former pushing for a further reduction of the property qualification, the latter demanding complete manhood suffrage. Townsend's version of *The Belly and the Members*, therefore, both looks back in its language to the 1640s and has been updated to meet the expectations of a now fully industrialized society. It begins by describing the rebellion of the members as a "solemn league and covenant," which was "kept as long as anything of that kind can be kept, which was until each of the rebel Members pined away to the skin and bone" (p. 123). But Townsend's central message was reserved for the "Application," in which he reminded his readers that the original fable was "celebrated as having been the means of appeasing a serious revolt and sedition in a crisis of peculiar danger to the Roman State." Significantly, Townsend makes no mention of Shakespeare's adaptation of the fable, not least, perhaps, because it was important to his case to retain the original structure of causation—not the famine on which *Coriolanus* had insisted, but instead resistance to taxation. And as for 1866, Townsend continued, "it is easy to see its application":

> For if the branches and members of a community refuse the government that aid which its necessities require, the whole must perish together. The story is of universal use. As the members of the human body have each their own function to discharge, so that no member can dispense with the service of the other, in like manner the connection of every class of society is required to the support and well-being of the whole. . . . The rich and the poor, the capitalist and the workman, render benefits to each other, and promote each other's welfare. In fact, the union of all classes is necessary to that maintenance of authority, respect for the public law, and stability of government, on which the safety of property to individuals and the continuance of the national prosperity alike depend.

It would be hard to find a more blatant example of organicist political theory transferred to a socioeconomic system for which a mechanical metaphor would seem, on the face of it, more appropriate. And, as a striking confirmation of Townsend's allegiances and intentions, it appears that, while eliding Shakespeare from this fable's cultural history, he had carefully consulted Ogilby. The "Application" ends, in fact, with a quotation (unidentified) from Ogilby's conclusion:

> The rich the poor, the poor the rich, should aid:
> None can protect themselves by their own shade.

More interesting figures than Townsend returned to the Body fable at this historical moment. It is not merely by coincidence that Marx himself was at this time thinking in terms of the Body fable, as, contemplating what others had called an "epidemic of strikes" throughout industrialized Europe, he entered an early challenge to the "laws" of classical economic theory, and specifically to the principle of fixity in real wages in relation to the gross national product. In *Value, Price and Profit*, written in 1865 though not published until 1898, Marx addressed himself to the "Citizens" of Europe and against John Weston, arguing for the legitimacy and efficacy of group protests in support of higher wages; and his argument was intended to show that wage levels were not fixed by absolute economic laws, but rather by "the *mere will* of the capitalist, or the limits of his avarice." "It is," wrote Marx, "an arbitrary limit. There is nothing necessary in it. It may be changed by the will of the capitalist, and may, therefore, be changed *against* his will"; and he proceeded to translate macroeconomic concepts back to their primal and most human origins—food and its distribution:

> Citizen Weston illustrated his theory by telling you that when a bowl contains a certain quantity of soup, to be eaten by a certain number of persons, an increase in the broadness of the spoons would not produce an increase in the amount of soup. He must allow me to find this illustration rather spoony. It reminded me somewhat of the simile employed by Menenius Agrippa. When the Roman plebeians struck against the Roman patricians, the patrician Agrippa told them that the patrician belly fed the plebeian members of the body politic. Agrippa failed to show that you feed the members of one man by filling the belly of another.[10]

One does not need to be a Marxist of any stamp (old, new, vulgar or literary-theoretical) to be struck by the wit of this application, and its cogent denial of such manifest untruths ("the capitalist and the workman . . . promote each other's welfare") as Townsend and others like him would produce and circulate.

But for my purposes, the most telling example of the Body fable's survival into a fully industrialized culture, with its increased need for acceptable myths (in Roland Barthes's sense of the word) is to be found in the territory of literature proper; very proper, as we shall see, and very literary, in the sense that its author connects the Body fable to cultural as well as to economic productivity and control. Like Townsend, George Eliot returned to *The Body and the Members* in formulating her position on the second Reform Bill, which in *Felix Holt* she chose to represent under the figure of the first Reform Bill of 1832. Published by the Tory publisher John Blackwood in June 1866, and subtitled *The Radical*, Eliot's novel features an artisanal hero who is proud of his working-class origins, and who actually finds himself leading a violent riot, for which he is imprisoned. Yet if we imagine that this premise would align Eliot on the populist side of the fable's history, or suppose that her earlier theological freethinking would have anticonservative political correlatives, we are soon disabused. The novel is devoted to the task of reconceiving radicalism in those safely interior, subjective, moral terms that, in Eliot's view, should render political change unnecessary, or so gradual in its arrival as not to be in the least upsetting. Initially defined pejoratively—"a Radical was no gentleman,"[11] Eliot's own position on further electoral reform is only slightly caricatured in an early statement: "Reform has set in by the will of the majority—that's the rabble, you know; and the respectability and good sense of the country, which are in the minority, are afraid of Reform running on too fast" (p. 188).

Unlike Townsend, Eliot chose not to ignore Shakespeare's version of the Body fable, but rather to reclaim it. Felix Holt is meant to emerge as the new, nineteenth-century Coriolanus, who will ultimately succeed better than his patrician predecessor by combining the role of tribune, man of the people, with the natural instincts of the patriciate. Felix's own credo is delivered (in a chapter that opens with an epigraph from Shakespeare's play, a heroic definition of Coriolanus) on nomination day. And Felix finds himself taking a heroic stance in the marketplace as the rhetorical opponent of a trades union speaker, who is arguing against Gladstone's limited Reform bill and for all of the demands of the People's Charter of 1838: "universal suffrage, and annual parliaments, and the vote by ballot, and electoral districts" (p. 397). This populist speech connects the issue of the franchise both with popular protest's primal fact, the fact of hunger, and with the ideological history of *The Body and the Members*:

> the greatest question in the world is, how to give every man a share in what goes on in life. . . . Not a pig's share, not a horse's share, not the share of machine fed with oil only to make it work and nothing else . . . that's a slave's share; we want a freeman's share, and that is to think and speak and act about what concerns us all, and see whether these fine gentlemen who undertake to govern us are doing the best they can for us. They've got the knowledge, say they. Very well, we've got the wants. There's many a one who would be idle if hunger didn't pinch him; but the stomach sets us to work. There's a fable told where the nobles are the belly and the people the members. But I make another sort of fable. I say, we are the belly that feels the pinches, and we'll set these aristocrats, these great people who call themselves our brains, to work at some way of satisfying us a bit better. (P. 396)

This unnamed speaker, evidently, is capable of rewriting Menenius Agrippa's fable so as to make it no longer inept but, on the contrary, an apt rationale for manhood suffrage, by connecting the primal urge to eat with the rational need to contribute rationally to the decisionmaking process that regulates, if not drives, the economy. But Felix Holt, eliding the materialist force of the fable, proceeds to express George Eliot's own doctrine that personal change, through education, should replace the demand for institutional or constitutional change:

> I want the working man to have power. I'm a working man myself, and I don't want to be anything else. But there are two sorts of power. There's a power to do mischief—to undo what has been done with great expense and labour, to waste and

destroy, to be cruel to the weak. . . . That's the sort of power that ignorant numbers have. . . . It's another sort of power that I want us working men to have, and I can see plainly enough that our all having votes will do little towards it at present. . . . I hope we, or the children that come after us, will get plenty of political power some time. But I should like to convince you that votes would never give you political power worth having while things are as they are now, and that if you go the right way to work you may get power sooner without votes. (P. 399)

Whatever meliorism, then, is to be aimed for, Felix declares, "must come out of human nature—out of men's passions, feelings, desires" (p. 400), which in turn will only be improved by sobriety and education.

Eliot's agenda was further clarified when, in response to an invitation by Blackwood to respond to the Second Reform Bill (and to Disraeli's "address to the working men" defending it), Eliot published in 1867 her own *Address to Working Men, by Felix Holt*, in which she again rewrote the fable of the Body in defense of her argument for organic growth rather than organized demand for change, and, in the process, clarified that slight shade of difference between her own position as novelist and intellectual from the more pragmatic concerns of G. F. Townsend. Starting from the premise (that was also Menenius Agrippa's in Shakespeare's play) that we all live with "the law of no man's making, and which no man can undo,"[12] and having as her objective the prevention of any further structural change, Eliot asserted that the organic health of England depends on the class structure. "Well," she wrote, "taking the world as it is . . . no society is made up of a single class: society stands before us like that wonderful piece of life, the human body, with all its various parts depending on one another, and with a terrible liability to get wrong because of that delicate dependence" (p. 615). Nothing is to be gained, therefore, but social disease, by "any attempt to do away directly with the actually existing class distinctions and advantages, as if everybody could have the same sort of work, or lead the same sort of life (which none of my hearers are stupid enough to suppose)" (pp. 616–17).

One might suppose such a statement incapable of repetition

today, even in England. But beyond this, Eliot acknowledged a form of elitism that has perhaps increased rather than diminished since the nineteenth century, and which transcends national boundaries. For the real wealth of the country, she suggested, consists in those intangible cultural treasures that only the upper classes possess: treasures "of knowledge, science, poetry, refinement of thought, feeling, and manners, great memories and the interpretation of great records, which is carried on from the minds of one generation to the minds of another" (p. 621). This cultural monopoly it was Eliot's intention to preserve; the Aesopian fable whose punch line Roland Barthes remembered also, not coincidentally, explained how the spoils of the hunt are reserved for the leader of the pack, rather than being equally distributed.

Such a program, of course, requires controlling the nature of the inheritance, deciding what constitutes a treasure and what is disposable rubbish. Almost every phrase in Eliot's statement helps to explain why she would have rejected the Aesopian tradition as I have defined it here: because its materialist and scatalogical myth of origins offends against "refinement of thought": because its approach to class makes the slave wittier than the master, the Negro more appealing than the Lion. And if, in its broadest sense, the canonical process can be equated with the storage of "great memories and the interpretation of great records," the problem to which Barthes pointed in his attempt to recover the meaning of "My name is lion," is one that did not develop by chance. Rather it was produced by centuries of effort, during which, from Plato's dialogues to Eliot's novels and beyond, the educational process, in cahoots with the political system, strove to keep the Aesopian tradition down.

■ Postscript

When Günter Grass introduced his own version of *Coriolanus*, *The Plebeians Rehearse the Uprising*, in an address to the Academy of Arts and Letters in Berlin on April 23, 1964, the occasion was the quatercentenary of Shakespeare's birth, the project an attack on Bertolt Brecht, the subject, once again, popular protest within a larger political framework. Brecht had himself attempted, in his own *Coriolan*, to make Shakespeare's play into an instrument of Marxist thought; for Grass (who believed this to be a serious distortion of Shakespeare's intentions) such an enterprise was rendered hypocritical by the failed East German industrial uprising of June 17, 1953, which Brecht notoriously had refused to support by any public statement. Brecht's *Coriolan* required, of course, a rewriting of the ancient Body fable; so Grass incorporated one of his own, allowing one of his characters to declare that *The Body and the Members* was still alive and well in modern political Europe. And this "nonsense hallowed by tradition" was not only effective against Shakespeare's plebeians, he argued, it was still operative as ideological suasion in modern East Germany. "The barbs of progress," wrote Grass with his provocative mixture of iconoclasm and conservativism, "cannot pierce its hide."[1]

Grass's application of *The Belly and the Members* to social structures in Cold War Europe is also instructive in what he took for granted: that the fable's organicist theory was so structured as to support Authority. Its "natural" message, Grass evidently believed, is against social disruption from below (in *The Plebeians Rehearse the Uprising*, against workers' protests) and not as a metaphor for a cooperative rhetoric from the left. At least this book has shown that premise to be false. But, in addition, I would like to believe, and bring some readers with me to that belief, that in a different sense from that intended by the author of "A Madrigall on Justice" in the 1640s, in the 1990s "The world is chang'd and we have Choyces" again. The extraordinary developments in Eastern Europe not only make it possible to proclaim that popular protest *can* succeed against seemingly impermeable autocracies ("The Lion's trod on by the Mouse") but render obsolete as explanations of historical events both Marxist theory and neoconservativism. No doubt they will survive as opinions; but between them clearly appears a new territory of theoretical compromise on the subject of the general will and the interanimation of the Body politic, a compromise which will have to be worked out most urgently in countries whose economic survival depends on it, but in which we can all participate. University professors have limited opportunities for such participation; but at least they could recover for their students the Aesopian tradition, in its adult political strength.

■ Notes

Introduction

1   Sir Francis Bacon, *Essayes or Counsels, Civill and Morall* (1625), in *Works*, ed. James Spedding, 14 vols. (London, 1857–74), 6:503.
2   Marcel Gutwirth, *Fable* (New Orleans, 1980), p. 3.
3   John Lydgate, *The Minor Poems*, ed. H. N. MacCracken, 2 vols. (London: EETS, 1934), 2:563.
4   Arnold Henderson, "Animal Fables as Vehicles of Social Protest and Satire: Twelfth Century to Henryson," *Third International Beast Epic, Fable and Fabliau Colloquium*, ed. Jay Goosens and Timothy Sodmann (Köln, 1981), p. 172.
5   Annabel Patterson, *Censorship and Interpretation* (Wisconsin, 1984).
6   Sir Roger L'Estrange, *Fables of Aesop and Other Eminent Mythologists; With Morals and Reflexions* (London, 1692), B1r.
7   This project converges with another of mine, on Shakespeare's supposedly antipopulist politics, where the chapter on *Coriolanus* also contains an extensive account of the Midlands Rising. The focus there, however, is less on Shakespeare's version of the Belly fable than on the meaning of the Coriolanus story, and of Roman republican history, as a whole.
8   Plato, *Phaedo*, 61, in *Euthyphro Apology Crito Phaedo Phaedrus*, trans. H. N. Fowler (London and Cambridge, Mass., 1914, Loeb edition), pp. 211–13.
9   Richard Mulcaster, *Elementarie* (1582), ed. E. T. Campagnac (Oxford, 1925), p. 14.
10 Roland Barthes, *Mythologies*, ed. and trans. Annette Lalvers (New York, 1972), pp. 115–16.
11 R. T. Lenaghan, ed., *Caxton's Aesop* (Cambridge, Mass., 1967), p. 77.
12 This was probably the *Aesopi vita & fabulae latine cum versione italica & allegoriis* published in Naples in 1483, which also contained the woodcuts from the 1480 Augsburg edition. See *The Literary Works of Leonardo da Vinci*, ed. Jean Paul Richter, 2 vols. (London, 1883, rev. 1939), 2:367–68.
13 Richter, ed., *The Literary Works of Leonardo da Vinci*, 2:27–286.
14 Kenneth Clarke, *Leonardo da Vinci* (Harmondsworth, England, 1958), p. 69.
15 Richter, ed., *The Literary Works of Leonardo da Vinci*, 2:279–80: "Usciendo un giorno il rasojo di quel manico, col quale si fa guaina a sé medesimo, e postosi al sole, vide il sole spechiarsi nel suo corpo; della qual cose prese somma gloria, e rivolto col pensiero indirieto cominciò con seco

medesimo a dire: Or tornerò io piu a qualla bottega della quale nova-
mente uscito sono? cierto no; non piaccia alli Dei che si splendida bellezza
caggia in tanta vilta d'animo! che pazzia sarebbe quella, la qual mi con-
ducesse a rader le insaponate barbe de' rustici villani a fare sì mecaniche
operationi! Or e questo corpo da simili eserciti? Cierto no; Io mi voglio
nascondere in qualche oculto loco, e li con tranquillo riposo passare mia
vita; E cosi nascosto per alquanti mesi, un giorno ritornato all'aria e uscito
fori della sua guaina, vidé se essere fatto a similitudine d'una rugginente
sega, e la sua superfitie non vi spechiare piu lo splendiente sole; con vano
pentimento indarno pianse lo inriparabile danno, con seco diciendo: o
quanto meglio era esercitare col barbiere il mio perduto taglio di tanta
sottilità; dov'è la lustrante superfitie? cierto la fastidiosa e brutta ruggine
l'à consumata!

1 Aesop's Life: Fathering the Fable

1   Paul de Man, "Dialogue and Dialogism," *Poetics Today* 4 (1983), p. 101; see
    G. W. F. Hegel, *Asthetik*, ed. G. Lukacs, 2 vols. (Frankfurt am Main, 1955),
    1:376.
2   William Caxton, *Fables of Esope* (1484), d8v. For a facsimile edition of Cax-
    ton's translation, see R. T. Lenaghan, ed., *Caxton's Aesop* (Cambridge, Mass.,
    1967), where this fable appears on p. 75.
3   Ben Edwin Perry, ed., *Aesopica*, 2 vols. (Urbana, 1952), 1:1–28. Hints in other
    classical authors, several of which may themselves be fictions, neverthe-
    less suggest that there was a "real" Aesop. See Perry, ed., *Aesopica*, 1:211–41;
    Babrius and Phaedrus (Cambridge, Mass., 1964, Loeb edition), pp. xxx–xlvi;
    and Emile Chambry, *Notice Sur Esope et les Fables Esopiques* (Paris, 1967), pp. ix–
    xxi. Herodotus (2:134–35), locating him in the 6th century B.C., was the
    source for Aesop's slavery and the manner of his death, but also for the
    statement of his relation to his beautiful fellow slave Rhodopis, an epi-
    sode omitted by Planudes. Aristotle (*Rhetoric*, 2:20:5–6) mentions Aesop's
    use of a fable (The Fox, Hedgehog, and Dog-fleas) in defense of a cer-
    tain Samian demagogue. Philostratus (*Imagines*, 1:3) describes a portrait of
    Aesop, surrounded by an audience of animals, and smiling.
4   L'Estrange, *Fables of Aesop and Other Eminent Mythologists: With Morals and Reflex-
    ions*, sig. A1r.
5   Joseph Jacobs, *The Fables of Aesop*, 3 vols. (New York, 1889, repr. 1970); 1:38–
    40.
6   Aldus Manutius, ed. and trans., *Vita (a Maximo Planude composita), & Fabellae
    Aesopi cum interpretatione Latina* (Venice, 1505).
7   For a more detailed account of Steinhöwel's collection see Lenaghan, ed.,
    Caxton's Aesop, pp. 1–24.

8   See Nicolaus Visscher, *The Labyrinth of Versailles* (Amsterdam, 1682).

9   Francis Barlow, *Aesop's Fables With His Life: in English, French and Latin* (London, 1687). This was a revised and more ornate version of Barlow's polyglot edition of 1666, *Aesop's Fables With His Life: In English, French & Latin. The English by Tho. Philipott Esq; The French and Latin by Rob. Codrington M.A. Ill. Francis Barlow* (London, 1666). Barlow's preface to the earlier version indicated that the work was engaged on "some years since," and the text indicates that it was a Royalist project. One competitor was the almost anonymous W. D. See *Aesop's Fables, with Their Morals in Prose and Verse, Grammatically Translated*, which by 1698 had reached its fourteenth edition. The sense of rivalry in Aesopian production is fully expressed in its preface, sig. A3r: "I here present thee with a new Edition of what thou hast already had; only a little larger, a little better, and the method a little alter'd. . . . But, Reader, I am to inform thee, that there came out lately a Paltry thing, just of the same shape and bigness with this Book in thy hand, and to compleat the cheat, it carries the same name, and hath counterfeited its Ornaments, the Pictures."

10 See Edward Hodnett, *Aesop in England: The Transmission of Motifs in Seventeenth-Century Illustrations of Aesop's Fables* (Charlottesville, Va., 1979), p. 63.

11 *Plutarch's Banquet of the Seven Sages*, trans. Jonathan Birch (London, 1833), p. 239. This translation, issued under the anagram Job Crithannah, accompanied *Fifty-One Original Fables* by the same author.

12 Barlow, *Aesop's Fables*, p. 1.

13 The attack on the legend of Aesop's ugliness was sometimes connected to his de-authorization. See Charles Bentley, *Dr. Bentley's Dissertation Upon the Fables of Aesop, Examin'd* (London, 1698), p. 283: "[Bentley] is extreamly concern'd to have Aesop thought Handsome, at the time that he is endeavouring all he can to prove him no Author. He hopes by his Civilities to his Person to atone for the Injuries he does him in his Writings: which is just such a compliment to Aesop's Memory, as it would be to Sir William Davenant's, should a man, in defiance of Common Fame, pretend to make out, that he had always a Good Nose in his Face; but, however, he did not write *Gondibert*."

14 See Mikhail Bakhtin, *Rabelais and His World*, trans. Helene Iswolsky (Boston, 1968, Bloomington, 1984), pp. 19–21.

15 Behn's verse is as follows:
    Oft for a jest we expose our modesty,
    And to assume a vertue, tell a ly,
    But here deceiving faire thou'dst small pretence,
    Thy Taile wants all but the kind feeling sense.

16 *Plutarch's Banquet*, p. 244.

17 This event, interestingly, occurs *before* he decodes the portent, but after he has read the social lesson of the corporal sign and its often more precious content.

18 The Neveletus/Anglicus text was a Latin versification of 58 fables from the first three books of the Romulus prose rescension. For a masterly summary of the enormously complex textual history of the Aesopian tradition, see Denton Fox, ed., *The Poems of Robert Henryson* (Oxford, 1981), pp. xli–xliii.

19 It is perhaps worth noting that Henryson's *couth*, or seemly, here and in the previous quotation, will subsequently (and unknowingly) be contradicted by Barlow's late seventeenth-century edition, where not only is the final violence directed against Aesop defined as "an uncouth crime" (p. 39), but the term is frequently used to define Aesop himself (pp. 7, 21, 23).

20 John Lydgate makes a comparable mistake. The Prologue to his *Isopes Fabules* describes how "the poete laureate/Callyd Isopus dyd hym occupy/Whylom in Rome to plese the senate,/Fond out fables, that men myght hem apply/To sondry matyrs, yche man for hys party." See John Lydgate, *The Minor Poems of John Lydgate*, ed. H. N. MacCracken, 2 vols. (London: EETS, 1934), 2:566–67. Lydgate, however, gives his Roman Aesop a connection with institutional politics, in his mention of "senate" and "party," that is as surprising as it is characteristic.

21 Fox, *The Poems*, p. 263.

22 Ibid.

23 Lydgate, *Minor Poems*, p. 577.

24 It is worth noting that Henryson's *Fables* were "Englished" and printed by Robert Smith in 1577.

25 Fox dismisses the proposal of Ranald Nicholson, in *Scotland: The Later Middle Ages* (Edinburgh, 1974), pp. 500–520, that the lion represented James III, the leading mouse represented Provost Walter Bertram, and the events were those of 1482, when the Edinburgh burgesses helped to obtain the release of the king from Edinburgh Castle. Fox believed that the "terms [of the fable] are so general as to make any allegorization improbable" (p. 264), and preferred the "convincing refutation" of R. J. Lyall, "Politics and Poetry in Fifteenth and Sixteenth Century Scotland," *Scottish Literary Journal* 3, no. 2 (1976): 7–10. This denial of topicality seems to run counter to Fox's brilliant account of the overall meaning of Henryson's selection and arrangement of his fables: that it illustrates the tragic ambivalence of Aesopian tradition with respect to its own powers of persuasion (lxxviii–lxxxi).

26 Méziriac, *La Vie d'Aesope, tirée des anciens auteurs* (Bourg-en-Bresse, 1632).

27 Robert Dodsley, *Fables of Aesop and Others* (Whitehaven, England, 1772), p. vii.

28 *The Fables of Aesop. With the moral reflections of Monsieur Baudoin. Translated . . . [by John Toland] To which is prefix'd by another hand; the true Life of Aesop, by . . . Monsieur de Méziriac*. (London, 1704).

29 See *The Fables of Jean de la Fontaine*, trans. Edward Marsh (London, 1933), p. xli.

30 Marie-Christine Bellosta, "La Vie d'Esope le Phrygien de La Fontaine ou les ruses de la vérité," Revue d'histoire littéraire de la France 79, no. 14 (1979): 5.

31 Compare Bellosta, "La Vie d'Esope," p. 6: "Quand il juge 'fabuleuse' la Vie de Planude, quand il estime que 'fable pour fable' elle vaut bien celle qu'il peut rediger lui-même, il ne faut pas comprendre ces termes au sens de 'mensongere, mensonge,' mais literalement: La Vie d'Esope le Phrygien par Jean de la Fontaine est la première des fables de son recueil."

32 Compare ibid., p. 7: "Il a omis aussi l'épisode que Baudoin intitule "subtile réponse d'Esope touchant les superfluités que la Nature rejette,' alors que cette réponse, explication, à laide d'un mythe de l'origine."

33 Ibid., p. 9: "Le lecteur des fables aura donc affaire à un discours qui supplée a l'impuissance qui frappe le discours rational quand il lui faut interpreter le monde. Le monde est d'ailleurs présenté, à travers l'anecdote de l'inscription ésoterique, comme un ensemble de signes dont le sens surabonde: Esope y lit trois textes possibles. Il est donc le découvreur de la multiplicité du sens des phénomènes. Et il reprend à son compte cette prolifération de la signification."

34 Compare ibid., p. 11: "Franche, la parole du fabuliste ne lui attire que des rigeurs, travestie par la drôlerie ou l'apologue, elle est la seule arme efficace de son impuissance esclave . . . La Vie d'Esope a pour principal point commun avec les autres fables de La Fontaine de montrer que la parole est le seul bien des faibles. . . . La Fontaine croit que le 'pouvoir des fables' peut suppléer un temps a l'impuissance réelle, . . . peut changer partiellement . . . le cours d'un monde sur lequel il n'exerce aucun pouvoir."

35 This is not the place for another analysis of the political meaning of La Fontaine's fables, which have been well described by Georges Couton, La Politique de La Fontaine (Paris, 1959), p. 11: "en rencontre dans les Fables des allusions transparentes à la politique étrangère. Les événements de la politique interieure ont laissé des reflets beaucoup moins discernables; une cryptographie à peu près indechiffrable les recouvre. Il s'y trouve encore une évocation extrêmement nuancée d'un climat politique et social. Il reste ainsi beaucoup plus facile de definir l'ensemble de la politique de La Fontaine, son état d'esprit et son humeur devant le fait politique que de préciser les intentions de chacque fable prise en particulier.

36 L. S. Vygotsky, The Psychology of Art, introd. A. N. Leontier, trans. Şcripta Technica (Cambridge, Mass., 1971), p. 110.

37 Vygotsky, Psychology, p. 107. The original is from Charles Batteux, Principes de Litterature, 5 vols. (Paris, 1764), 2:1:5.

38 Vygotsky, Psychology of Art, p. 133.

39 Marcel Gutwirth, Fable (New Orleans, 1980), p. 3: "Nothing indeed is quite so dead as the standard Aesopian collection." Gutwirth's point, however, was that the genre, "consigned to cold storage" by didacticism, never-

theless mysteriously resisted this destructive process and was still alive "when La Fontaine, brushing away the dust of ages of misuse, chose to train upon animal fable the sparkle of his wit" (p. 4).

2 Fables of Power: The Sixteenth Century

1 For the different versions of the story, originating in the Latin *Disciplina clerica* of Petrus Alfonsi, see J. O. Halliwell, ed., *Lydgate's Minor Poems*, in *Early English Poetry, Ballads, and Popular Literature*, 2 vols. (London: Percy Society, 1940), 2:179.

2 John Lydgate, *The Minor Poems*, ed. H. N. MacCracken, 2 vols. (London: EETS, 1934), 2:472. It appears that Sir Thomas Wyatt remembered these lines when imprisoned by Henry VIII in 1541, subsequent to Thomas Cromwell's fall from power and influence. Wyatt wrote to his friend Sir Francis Brian: "Syghes ar my foode, drynke are my teares; / Clynkinge of fetters such musycke wolde crave"; and in another related poem, he ironically contrasted his incarcerated self to that of his own hunting birds: "Luckes, my faire falcon, and your fellowes all, / How well plesaunt yt were your libertiee!" See Sir Thomas Wyatt, *Collected Poems*, ed. Kenneth Muir (London, 1949), pp. 159, 160.

3 Gotthold Lessing, *Abhandlungen über die Fabel*, in *Gesammelte Werke*, vol. 1 (Berlin and Weimar, 1981), pp. 359–60. The fable in question here was *The Horse, the Hunter, and the Hart* (Romulus, 4:9), in which the horse "allowed itself to be bridled by the man . . . in order to revenge himself on the deer." As Lessing complained, this fable became allegorical by its occasion, as related by Stesichorus, "at a time when the Himerenses had made Phalaris the commander of their forces, and were about to furnish him with a body guard" (Aristotle, *Rhetoric*, 2:20). "All is here allegorical," Lessing complained, "but only because . . . the bridle [is not made applicable] to every first encroachment upon liberty, but simply to the unrestricted commandership of Phalaris."

4 See chapter 1, pp. 33–34.

5 Derek Pearsall, *John Lydgate* (London, 1970), pp. 197, 196, 194–95. These views are largely repeated by Lois Eben, *John Lydgate* (Boston, 1985), pp. 105–11.

6 Geoffrey Chaucer, *Works*, ed. F. N. Robinson (Cambridge, Mass., 1957), pp. 225–27.

7 Quotation from *John Skelton: The Complete English Poems* (London, 1983). For an argument that Skelton wrote *Speke, Parott* as a bid for renewed royal favor, and that he badly miscalculated Wolsey's capacity to survive, see Greg Walker, *John Skelton and the Politics of the 1520s* (Cambridge, 1988), pp. 88–100.

8 Arthur Kinney, *John Skelton: Priest as Poet* (Chapel Hill, N.C., 1987), pp. 15–30.

9 Malcolm Andrew, ed., *Two Early Renaissance Bird Poems: The Harmony of Birds, The Parliament of Birds* (London and Toronto, 1984), p. 59.

10 See "Howe Collingbourne was cruelly executed for making a foolishe rime," in Richard III's reign, specifically for not remembering to "Touche covertly in termes," but for writing a poem in which "The Cat, the Rat, and Lovel our Dog, / Do rule al England, under a Hog," whereof, Collingbourne complains, "the meanyng was so playne and true, / That every foole perceyved it." *The Mirror for Magistrates*, ed. Lily B. Campbell (New York, 1960), pp. 347, 349.

11 For an account of the poem as an extended satire on the ministry of Burghley's son, Robert Cecil, from Donne's perspective as a supporter of Ralegh and ambivalent toward Essex, both of whom could be seen as Cecil's victims, see M. van Wyk Smith, "John Donne's *Metempsychosis*," *Review of English Studies* n.s. 24 (1973): 17–25, 141–52.

12 For the texts, in order cited, see John Donne, *Poetical Works*, ed. H. J. Grierson, 2 vols. (Oxford, 1912), 1:171, 178, 78. The epigram was directed against the newssheet, *Mercurius Bello-Gallicus*, which Donne regarded as a source of misinformation.

13 For Jonson's return to the beast epic of *Reynard the Fox* (one branch of which was also translated by Caxton in 1481), see R. B. Parker, "*Volpone* and *Reynard the Fox*," *Review of English Studies* n.s. 1 (1950): 242–44. Parker provides an invaluable summary of the evolution and dispersal of the Reynard legends, and shows how Jonson's play shares the confusion of tone endemic to medieval tales "which all commentators see as a tug-of-war between an anarchic identification with the fox and a satiric condemnation of the evils and institutions he represents" (p. 35).

14 Raphael Holinshed, *Chronicles of England, Scotland and Ireland* 6 vols. (London, 1808; repr. New York, 1965), 4:912.

15 Lenaghan, ed., *Caxton's Aesop*, p. 126.

16 On this transition, and the collapse of aristocratic dissidence into passive obedience to the monarchy, see K. B. McFarlane, "The Wars of the Roses," in *England in the Fifteenth Century: Collected Essays*, intro. G. L. Harriss (London, 1981), pp. 87–119, 260; and Mervyn James, *Society, Politics and Culture: Studies in Early Modern England* (Cambridge, 1986).

17 Compare Holinshed, *Chronicles*, 4:916, on the meaning of the crowds at the execution: "although the assemblie were woonderfull great, and the traitors all goodlie personages, clothed in silkes, &c: and everie waie furnished to moove pitie . . . yet . . . there appeared no sadnesse or alteration among the people, at the mangling and quartering of their bodies."

18 See Elizabeth Story Donno, "Some Aspects of Shakespeare's Holinshed," *Huntington Library Quarterly* 50 (1987): 229–47.

19 Edmund Spenser, *Poetical Works*, ed. J. C. Smith and E. de Selincourt (London, 1912), p. 417.

20 See Annabel Patterson, *Pastoral and Ideology* (Berkeley, Calif., 1987), pp. 49–57.

21 While Spenser usually refers to the Lion as male, there is one line (629) in which her female sex slips through the convention.

22 In fact, these two fables are only the frame for an extended critique on Elizabethan society, including more than 100 lines of anticlerical satire, and an even longer diatribe on how knaves succeed at court and the miseries of clientage. "What hell it is," wrote Spenser, "in suing long to bide . . . To have thy Princes grace, yet want her Peeres" (ll. 895, 900).

23 For this long-standing interpretation, as well as a theory that the *Tale* was composed in two parts, one in 1579–80, the other in 1591, see Edwin Greenlaw, *Studies in Spenser's Historical Allegory* (Baltimore, 1932), pp. 112–24.

24 Richard Bancroft, *A Survey of the Pretended Holy Discipline* (London, 1593), pp. 8–9.

25 See H. S. V. Jones, *A Spenser Handbook* (New York, 1930), pp. 74–75, who lists references to the "calling-in" by Gabriel Harvey (1592), Thomas Nashe (1593), John Weever (1599), and Thomas Middleton (1604). Jones adds that the *Tale* was omitted from the Folio of 1611, presumably to avoid offending Burghley's son, Sir Robert Cecil, but that it reappeared in editions following Cecil's death in 1611.

26 For the text see Jean Robertson, ed., *The Countess of Pembroke's Arcadia* (Oxford, 1973), pp. 254–59.

27 For a clear account of this theory and its chief exponents, see J. P. Sommerville, *Politics and Ideology in England, 1603–1640* (London and New York, 1986), pp. 64–85.

28 There is disagreement as to Sidney's attitude toward the "commons," and especially toward popular protest, as articulated in the *Arcadia*. Compare Stephen Greenblatt, "Murdering Peasants," *Representations* 1 (1983): 1–29; and Richard M. Berrong, "Changing Depictions of Popular Revolt in Sixteenth-Century England: The Case of Sidney's Two *Arcadias*," *Journal of Medieval and Renaissance Studies* 19 (1989): 15–33.

29 This fable has occasioned much scholarly dispute as to its meaning. For a recent summary of previous arguments (as well as a proposal, with which I disagree, that the fable rejects the antimonarchism of Hubert Languet), see Martin N. Raitiere, *Sir Philip Sidney and Renaissance Political Theory* (Pittsburgh, 1984), pp. 57–101.

30 This concept Aesop himself articulates in his first fable as delivered to the Samians: in the words of the *Life*, the fabulist reconstructs what it was like "In elder Times when Beasts had speech."

31 See Andrew, ed., *Two Early Renaissance Bird Poems*, p. 26.

32 Sidney, *Old Arcadia*, pp. 78–79.

33 John Lyly, *Euphues and His England* (London, 1609), p. 39. There were previous editions in 1579, 1580, 1582, 1586, 1597, 1606, and several more in the reigns of both James I and Charles I. Whether one understands such

a publication history as proof of a work's popularity or of its political usefulness, it is worth noting that *Euphues and His England* continued to be republished long after the fashion for Euphuism had become a subject for mockery.

34 Since Lyly shared with antiquity the belief that bees were ruled by a king, not a queen, he missed an opportunity to "apply" his natural history to Elizabeth in a gender-specific way. This opportunity was first used in the 1630s in relation to Henrietta Maria. But in Lyly's case the resulting masculinization merely matches his strategy in the fable of the lion, the wolf, and the fox (as was also the case in *Mother Hubberds Tale*). There seems to have been no attempt in Elizabethan fables to adapt their protagonists' sex to the special circumstances of a female monarch.

3 "The Fable Is Inverted": 1628–1700

1 See Hoyt Hudson, "John Hepwith's Spenserian Satire upon Buckingham: With Some Jacobean Analogues," *Huntington Library Bulletin* 6 (1934): 39–71.

2 Robert Johnson et al., eds., *Commons Debates 1628*, 5 vols. (New Haven, Conn., and London, 1977), 3:532.

3 Lenaghan, ed., *Caxton's Aesop*, p. 77.

4 *Aesop's Fables, with Their Morals in Prose and Verse, Grammatically Translated*, 14th ed. (London, 1698), p. 7.

5 Mary H. Pritchard, "Fables Moral and Political: The adaptation of the Aesopian Fable Collection to English Social and Political Life, 1651–1722" (unpublished Ph.D. dissertation, University of Western Ontario, Canada, 1976), pp. 36–37.

6 For Ogilby's biography, see Katherine Van Eerde, *John Ogilby and the Taste of His Times* (Folkestone, England, 1976); and see also Marion Eames, "John Ogilby and His Aesop," *Bulletin of the New York Public Library* 65 (1961): 73–78; Earl Miner's facsimile edition of the 1668 *Fables* (Los Angeles: Augustan Reprint Society, 1965), pp. i–xiv; Margret Schuchard, *John Ogilby, 1660–1676; Lebenbild eines Gentleman mit vielen Karieren* (Hamburg, 1973).

7 For Engagement politics see David Underdown, *Royalist Conspiracy in England, 1649–1660* (New Haven, Conn., 1960), pp. 30–51, 73–96.

8 Compare, however, Philip Massinger's play, *The Emperor of the East*, which appeared in 1631–32, at the beginning of Charles I's period of prerogative rule, and whose fictional protagonist complains:
... O the miserable
Condition of a Prince! who though hee varie
More shapes than Proteus in his minde, and manners,
Hee cannot winne an universall suffrage,
From the many-headed Monster, Multitude.
Like Aesops foolish Frogges they trample on him

As a senselesse blocke, if his government bee easie.

And if he prove a Storke, they croke, and rayle

Against him as a tyranne.

See *The Plays and Poems of Philip Massinger*, ed. Philip Edwards and Colin Gibson, 5 vols. (Oxford, 1976), p. 428.

9 John Milton, *Complete Prose Works*, ed. D. M. Wolfe et al., 8 vols. (New Haven, Conn., 1953–80), 7:748.

10 Andrew Marvell, *The Poems and Letters*, ed. H. M. Margoliouth, rev. Pierre Legouis, 2 vols. (Oxford, 1971), 1:179, 212.

11 John Freke, *The History of Insipids*, in *Anthology of Poems on Affairs of State*, ed. George de F. Lord (New Haven, Conn., and London, 1975), p. 143.

12 John Dryden, "The Hind and the Panther," pt. 3, l. 1198, in *Poems 1685–1692*, ed. Earl Miner and Vincent Dearing, in *Works*, 20 vols. (Berkeley and Los Angeles, 1956–87), vol. 3 (1969).

13 In *Dryden's Poetry* (Bloomington, Ind., and London, 1967), pp. 157, 339, Earl Miner points out that the text is sprinkled with other, less obvious allusions to fables, and that in one passage (1:438–47) there are three allusions within ten lines, to *The Husbandman and the Wood*, *The Gourd and the Pine*, and *The Sun, the Wind, and the Traveller*.

14 Miner's commentary is available both in his notes to the edition, cited above, and in *Dryden's Poetry*, pp. 144–205.

15 John Ogilby, *The Fables of Aesop Paraphras'd in Verse*, Fable 9.

16 John Locke, *Two Treatises of Government*, ed. Peter Laslett (Cambridge, 1967), p. 169. For Laslett's argument about dating see pp. 45–66.

17 Dryden, *Works*, 3:161.

18 Dryden, *Absalom and Achitophel*, cited from *Poems 1681–1684*, ed. H. T. Swedenberg, Jr., in *Works*, vol. 2 (1972).

19 Steven Zwicker, *Politics and Language in Dryden's Poetry: The Arts of Disguise* (Princeton, 1984), pp. 123–58.

20 Ibid., p. 164.

4 Body Fables

1 William Camden, *Remaines of a Greater Worke, concerning Britaine* (London, 1605), pp. 198–99.

2 Plutarch, *The Lives of the Noble Grecians and Romaines*, trans. Thomas North (London, 1603), pp. 223–24.

3 For the "Epistle Apologeticall" and an account of the circumstances, see Margaret Dowling, "Sir John Hayward's Troubles Over His Life of Henry IV," *The Library*, 4th series, 11 (1930–31): 221–22.

4 Edward Forset, *A Comparative Discourse of the Bodies Natural and Politique* (London, 1606), pp. 100, 15, 58.

5 Philip Brockbank, ed., *Coriolanus* (London, 1976), p. 39.

6   See W. Gordon Zeefeld, "'Coriolanus' and Jacobean Politics," *Modern Language Review* 17 (1962): 327–28; and C. C. Huffman, *Coriolanus in Context* (Lewisburg, Penn., 1971), pp. 147–50.

7   See James F. Larkin and Paul L. Hughes, eds., *Stuart Royal Proclamations*, 2 vols. (Oxford, 1973), 1:153 n.1.

8   See David Underdown, *Revel, Riot and Rebellion: Popular Politics and Culture in England 1603–1660* (Oxford, 1985), p. 115.

9   See Andrew Charlesworth, ed., *An Atlas of Rural Protest in Britain 1548–1900* (Philadelphia, 1983), pp. 33–34.

10   Larkin and Hughes, *Stuart Royal Proclamations*, 1:155 n.2.

11   See Joan Thirsk, *The Agrarian History of England and Wales (1500–1640)*, 8 vols. (Cambridge, 1967), 4:820.

12   Larkin and Hughes, *Stuart Royal Proclamations*, 1:161.

13   *Orders Appointed by his Majestie to be straigtly observed for the preventing and remedying of the dearth of Graine and other Victuall.* June 1, 1608 (London, 1608), p. 13.

14   Larkin and Hughes, *Stuart Royal Proclamations*, 1:202.

15   One can be confident of using this phrase when proclamations are involved, since their very function is to bring to public consciousness a particular aspect of governmental policy.

16   Charles Gildon, *Remarks on the Plays of Shakespeare in Works of Shakespeare*, ed. Rowe, vol. 7 (London, 1710), pp. 362–63.

17   Günter Grass, *The Plebeians Rehearse the Uprising*, trans. Ralph Manheim (New York, 1966), p. xii.

18   E. C. Pettet, "Coriolanus and the Midlands Insurrection of 1607," *Shakespeare Survey* 3 (1950): 39.

19   E. P. Thompson, "The Moral Economy of the English Crowd in the Eighteenth Century," *Past and Present* 50 (1971): 76–136.

20   For an account of this manuscript, B. L. Harleian 5106, see James Spedding, ed., *The Works of Francis Bacon*, 14 vols. (London, 1857–74), 6:535.

21   Francis Bacon, *Essayes or Counsels, Civill and Morall* (London, 1625), in *Works*, 6:409.

22   Robert Wilkinson, *A Sermon Preached at North-Hampton the 21 of June last past, before the Lord Lieutenant of the County, and the rest of the Commissioners there assembled upon occasion of the late Rebellion and Riots in those parts committed. Pro.22.2 The rich & the poore meete together, the Lord is the maker of them all* (London, 1607).

23   See Elizabeth Read Foster, ed., *Proceedings in Parliament 1610*, 2 vols. (New Haven, Conn., 1966), 2:10–11.

24   *The Kings Majestie's Speach To the Lords and Commons . . . on Wednesday the xxi of March, Anno Dom. 1609* (London, 1610), B2.

25   See Foster, *Proceedings in Parliament 1610*, 1:268.

26   John Milton, *Of Reformation Touching Church Discipline in England*, in *Prose Works*, ed. D. M. Wolfe et al., 8 vols. (New Haven, Conn., 1953–82), 1:583.

27   "A Madrigall on Justice," in *Rump: or, an Exact Collection of the Choycest Poems*

and Songs Relating to the Late Times, 2 vols. (1662, repr. London, 1874), 1:36.

28 John Ogilby, Fables of Aesop Paraphras'd in Verse (London, 1651), p. 13.

29 Michel Foucault, Power/Knowledge (New York, 1980), p. 97.

30 Thomas Hobbes, Leviathan, ed. C. B. Macpherson (Harmondsworth, England, 1968), pp. 300–301.

31 Peter Laslett, ed., John Locke: Two Treatises of Government (Cambridge, 1967; 2d ed.), pp. 3–4.

32 See John Harrison and Peter Laslett, The Library of John Locke (Oxford, 1971; 2d ed.), p. 69.

33 Locke, Works, Some Thoughts Concerning Education, ed. F. W. Garforth (New York, 1964), pp. 189–190.

5 "The World Is Chang'd": 1700–2000

1 See George Kitchin, Sir Roger L'Estrange: A Contribution to the History of the Press in the Seventeenth Century (London, 1913), p. 397. L'Estrange fought for Charles I, and was imprisoned for four years for his efforts to recapture Lynn in Norfolk for the king. In 1660 he attacked Milton in No Blind Guides, and he subsequently attacked the author of The Growth of Popery and Arbitrary Government whom he rightly suspected to be Andrew Marvell.

2 L'Estrange's collection was an eclectic one, compiled from Phaedrus, Camerarius, Avianus, Neveletus, Apthonius, Babrias, Baudoin, La Fontaine, Aesope en Belle Humeur, etc.

3 Much of Phaedrus's biography remains conjectural, but one of the principal manuscripts of his fables states that he was made a freedman by Augustus, and various autobiographical hints in the fables place him as living under Tiberius. See Ben Edwin Perry, ed., Babrius and Phaedrus (Cambridge, Mass., 1964, Loeb edition), pp. lxiii–lxxxii.

4 Although L'Estrange and Croxall were the strongest and clearest representatives of this development, they were not its only exponents. Other examples include the Restoration collections Aesop Explained (1672), and Aesop Improved (1673); the polyglot editions which began in 1666 and continued through 1687, with a mild but discernible pro-Stuart bias; Nathaniel Crouch's Delightful Fables of 1691, which were decisively Whig and Williamite, and which in some later editions appeared, as in 1712, as Aesop's Fables; and Aesop Naturaliz'd and Expos'd To the Publick View In his Own Shape and Dress (Cambridge, 1697), whose targets are, as well as politicians, projectors, court flatterers, taxes, beaux, and landlords.

5 Mary H. Pritchard, "Fables Moral and Political: The Adaptation of the Aesopian Fable Collection to English Social and Political Life, 1651–1722" (unpublished Ph.D. dissertation, University of Western Ontario, Canada, 1976), pp. 177–78.

6   *Aesop the Wanderer: Or, Fables Relating to the Transactions of Europe; Occasionally Writ since the Battle of Blenheim* (London, 1704 [August 31]), p. 7.

7   *Aesop in Downing Street* (London, 1831), pp. 4–5.

8   G. F. Townsend, *The Fables of Aesop, with New Applications, Morals, etc.* (London, 1866), fable xxv, p. 56.

9   Ibid., p. 123.

10 Karl Marx, *Value, Price and Profit*, in *Collected Works* (New York, 1985), 20:104, 106.

11 George Eliot, *Felix Holt, The Radical*, ed. Peter Coveney (Harmondsworth, England, 1972), p. 56.

12 See *Felix Holt*, ed. Coveney, Appendix A, p. 613.

Postscript

1   Grass, *The Plebeians Rehearse the Uprising*, pp. 80–81.

▪ Index

About the Author. Annabel Patterson is Professor of English and
Professor in the Graduate Program in Literature at Duke
University. Previous publications include *Censorship and
Interpretation*, *Hermogenes and the Renaissance: Seven Ideals of Style*,
Marvel and the Civic Crown, *Pastoral and Ideology: Virgil to Valéry*, and
Shakespeare and the Popular Voice.

Library of Congress Cataloging-in-Publication Data
Patterson, Annabel M.
Fables of power : Aesopian writing and political history /
Annabel Patterson.
(Post-contemporary interventions)
Includes bibliographical references and index.
ISBN 0-8223-1106-2 (cloth).—ISBN 0-8223-1118-6 (paper)
1. English literature—Early modern, 1500–1700—History and
criticism. 2. Politics and literature—Great Britain—History—
16th century. 3. Politics and literature—Great Britain—
History—17th century. 4. Political fiction, English—History
and criticism. 5. Political poetry, English—History and
criticism. 6. Great Britain—Politics and government—1485–
1603. 7. Great Britain—Politics and government—1603–1714. 8.
Aesop's fables—Parodies, imitations, etc. 9. Fables, English—
History and criticism. 10. English literature—Greek influences.
11. Aesop—Influence. I. Title. II. Series.
PR428.P6P38 1991
820.9′358—dc20   90-46299   CIP